Business
Banking

English Language Services, Inc.

Consultant: William A. Mundell, MBA

MACMILLAN PUBLISHING CO., INC.
New York

COLLIER MACMILLAN INTERNATIONAL
A Division of Macmillan Publishing Co., Inc.

COLLIER MACMILLAN PUBLISHERS
London

ACKNOWLEDGEMENTS

Photography Credits: Leo de Wys, Inc.: © E.C. Johnson, © Vannucci; Courtesy of Federal Reserve System; Monkmeyer Press Photo Service: © Mimi Forsyth, © Freda Leinwand; Photo Researchers, Inc.: © Rhoda Galyn, © Guy Gillette, © Robert Houser, © Paolo Koch, Rapho, © Bettye Lane, © Sherry Suris, Rapho, © Waagenaar, Rapho; Stock, Boston: © Ellis Herwig; © Strix Pix; Taurus Photos: © Russell A. Thompson.

Cover Design Rudy Michaels

Cover Photo © E. Johnson from Leo de Wys, Inc.

Bank documents courtesy of: The Bank of New York
The Chase Manhattan Bank, N.A.

Parts of this work were published in the text, Special English: Banking.

Macmillan Publishing Co., Inc.
866 Third Avenue, New York, N.Y. 10022
Collier Macmillan Canada, Inc.

Printed in the United States of America

ISBN 0-02-973650-1

9 8 7 6 5 4 3 2 1

Preface

This book is one of Macmillan's *Career English* series. *Career English* is intended for students who have some proficiency in English as well as a working knowledge of their own professional fields. The books are designed to teach the special terminology students need in order to communicate in English within their career areas.

Students will find the *Career English* books clear, lively, practical, and easy to use. Each chapter covers one specific topic and begins with a dialogue between an expert in the field and a student or a trainee. In the course of the dialogue, the key terms pertaining to the chapter topic are introduced in a realistic context. The dialogue is followed by a terminology practice in which each key term is defined and used in three sample sentences. At the end of each chapter, students will find a simple check-up exercise to determine whether or not they have mastered the terms introduced in the dialogue. An answer key to the check-ups is provided for self-correction. A glossary at the end of each book lists all the terms in the text with the numbers of the chapters in which they appear. In addition a cassette recording of the dialogues is available for each book. Use of the cassette is optional but highly recommended.

The books in the *Career English* series are designed to be equally useful for students studying in a classroom or independently.

To the student: If you are studying independently, the following suggestions will help you to use this book to its best advantage:

1. Read the dialogue from beginning to end.
2. Read the terminology practice.
3. If you have the tape, listen to it. Listen for the words in the terminology practice, paying special attention to pronunciation and intonation.
4. Reread the dialogue aloud. (If you have the tape, play it again to check your pronunciation.)
5. Do the end-of-chapter check-up to be sure you have mastered the terms introduced in the chapter. Check your answers with the answer key at the back of the book. If you have made an error in the check-up, use the terminology practice to look up the words you have not mastered. Find the terms in the dialogue, and reread the dialogue. Correct your errors.
6. Now you are ready to go on to the next chapter.

To the teacher: The following suggestions will help you to use this book to its best advantage in your classroom:

1. Ask students to read the dialogue silently.
2. Have them read the terminology practice to themselves.
3. If you have the tape, play it for the class. Suggest that students follow along in their books, listening carefully for the words in the terminology practice and paying careful attention to pronunciation and intonation.
4. Read each word in the terminology practice aloud, asking students to repeat after you. Check for pronunciation. Have students take turns reading the sample sentences aloud.
5. Ask two students to read the dialogue aloud, taking the parts of the characters in the dialogue. (You may wish to have several pairs of students read each dialogue.) As the dialogue is being read, help the students with their pronunciation and intonation.
6. Ask students to do the end-of-chapter check-up to be sure they have mastered the vocabulary introduced in the chapter. If students have their own books, they may write their answers directly in the book. If the books will be used by others, ask students to write their answers on separate paper.
7. Students can check their answers with the answer key at the back of the book. If they have made any errors, suggest they look up the terms in the terminology practice, reread the definitions and sample sentences, and reread the dialogue. Then have them correct their check-ups.

CONTENTS

Lesson page

1 Structure and Functions of a Bank 1

2 Currency and Other Forms of Exchange . . . 6

3 Checking Accounts 14

4 Time Deposits, Savings Accounts, and NOW Accounts 18

5 Loans (1) 23

6 Loans (2) 27

7 Bank Investments 32

8 Types of Banking Institutions 37

9 Trust Services 42

10 Brokerage Services 47

11 Interbank Relations 52

12 The Federal Reserve System 56

13 Government Controls 62

14 The Eurodollar Market 68

Key to Exercises 72

Appendix 75

Glossary 78

LESSON

Structure and Functions of a Bank

A. Dialogue

Customer: Who really owns the bank?

Banker: The stockholders own it. In the beginning, they put up the necessary capital and were granted a charter from either a state or local government.

Customer: Are the members of the board of directors stockholders?

Banker: Oh, yes. They're chosen by the other stockholders to operate the bank.

Customer: And the board hires the president and the vice-presidents to manage it.

Banker: That's right. Along with the cashier, the tellers, and the clerical workers.

Customer: I guess most of your work has to do with checking and savings accounts and making loans.

Banker: Yes. But we invest money, too. Planning the bank's investments is also very important.

Customer: Do you divide all the profits among the stockholders?

Banker: Not all of them. The stockholders receive regular dividends. But some of our earnings are held in reserve accounts.

Customer: I suppose that would be necessary.

Banker: Here's a copy of our last published statement. You see, the reserves are shown here as surplus and undivided profits.

B. Terminology Practice

account: in this sense, a record of financial **transactions***; money on deposit in a bank

I guess your work has to do with checking accounts.
We've had an account with them for years.
You don't make much on that kind of account.

board of directors: a group of people who control the activities of a bank or company

Are the members of the board of directors stockholders?
When will the board of directors meet?
He's a member of the board of directors.

capital: in this sense, the money used to start a bank or company

They put up the necessary capital.
What is the amount of the capital?
They had some trouble raising the capital.

cashier: an officer of a bank in charge of the money which goes in and out of a bank or company

They hire the president and vice-president, along with the cashier.
You'd better see the cashier about that.
The cashier is on vacation just now.

* Words in boldface type appear in the glossary.

charter: in this sense, permission granted by the government to do business

They were granted a charter by the government.
When was the charter granted?
I don't think they'll be able to get a charter.

checking account: an account in a bank from which money can be drawn by **check**

I guess your work has to do with checking accounts.
How much money is left in my checking account?
I'd like to close my checking account.

clerical: having to do with the keeping of records and with correspondence

The board hires them, along with the clerical workers.
We're behind on our clerical work.
Do you have any clerical jobs open now?

dividend: a sum of money paid to a stockholder or shares of **stock** issued to him out of profits in relation to his investment

The stockholders receive regular dividends.
The last dividend was quite large.
How much did you receive in dividends?

invest: put money into a business in order to make a profit

Yes, but we invest money, too.
I'd like to invest in some mutual bonds.
How much money does she have to invest?

investment: money put into a business in order to make profit; the act of doing this

Planning the bank's investments is very important.
I want to talk to you about my investments.
Would you make an investment of that kind?

loan: in this sense, money which one person allows another to use for a specified time and which will be returned with an additional payment for its use; the act of giving out such money

I guess your work has to do with making loans.
He's afraid he's made a bad loan.
What is the amount of the loan?

president: the officer who has the major responsibility for the management of a business

The board hires the president and the vice-presidents.
This decision will have to be made by the president.
Doesn't that company have a new president?

profit: earnings remaining after all the expenses of a business activity have been paid

Do you divide all the profits among the stockholders?
We expect to make a nice profit this year.
The profits have been slowly rising.

reserves: in this sense, earnings kept back for later use

Some of our earnings are held in reserve accounts.
Their reserves are getting pretty low.
They were lucky to have such large reserves.

savings account: an account in a bank on which the **depositor** receives **interest**

I guess your work has to do with savings accounts.
They have a savings account with us.
He decided to put the money in a savings account.

statement: in this sense, an announcement of a bank's financial condition

Here's a copy of our last published statement.
You have every reason to be proud of this statement.
Our new statement will be published next week.

stockholder: a **party** who holds part ownership in a company

The stockholders own it.
The statement will be sent to all the stockholders.
He's one of our largest stockholders.

surplus: money owned by a company in addition to its capital

The reserves are shown here as surplus and undivided profits.
The surplus is now as large as the capital.
They've built up a nice surplus.

teller: an employee in a bank who pays out and receives money

The board hires them, along with the tellers.
Take this to one of the tellers' windows.
The teller took the problem to the cashier.

undivided profits: profits not yet paid out as dividends or added to the surplus

The reserves are shown here as surplus and undivided profits.
I didn't know the undivided profits were this high.
How much undivided profit do you have?

vice-president: an officer in a company who assists the president

The board hires the president and the vice-presidents.
This department is supervised by a vice-president.
One of the vice-presidents can handle this matter.

C. Check-Up

Fill in the blanks with the proper terms from the list.

board of directors	profits
capital	reserves
dividends	statement
investments	stockholders
loan	vice-president

1. The men who control the activities of the bank will meet today. The ______ will meet.
2. They were chosen by all the parties who hold part ownership in the bank. They were chosen by the ______.
3. The board will discuss the hiring of a person to assist the president. They must hire a new ______.
4. They'll also discuss the new announcement of the bank's financial condition. They'll discuss the ______.
5. Then they must make a decision about the earnings they're keeping back for later use. They must decide what to do about the ______.
6. This is money held by the bank in addition to the amount the stockholders put up to start the bank. It's money held in addition to the ______.
7. The board may want to pay some money to the stockholders out of profits. They may give out ______.
8. Quite a lot of money was left over this year after all the bank's expenses were paid. The ______ were high.
9. The president will ask the board to approve a large ______ to a customer. This is money owned by the bank which the customer will be permitted to use for a time and then return with an additional payment for its use.
10. The board will probably discuss the money which the bank has put into other businesses in order to make profits. They'll discuss the bank's ______.

LESSON

Currency and Other Forms of Exchange

A. Dialogue

Student: The bank must use just about every form of exchange in a day's work.

Cashier: Just about. Of course, we constantly handle coins and bills of every denomination.

Student: They're what you call legal tender.

Cashier: Yes. Or currency. A nation's currency is its legal tender.

Student: But a check isn't legal tender.

Cashier: No. However, checks are a more common form of exchange. The Federal Reserve Board defines checkable deposits as one of the most important sources of the money supply.

Student: Are traveler's checks currency?

Cashier: Not in a strict sense. But they're immediately negotiable everywhere. For instance, even merchants will cash them under most circumstances.

Student: The bearer need only present proper identification.
Cashier: That's right.
Student: Well, what's a bank note? Is that currency?
Cashier: Definitely. Bank notes are issued by the banks of the Federal Reserve System, and they're legal tender just as silver certificates are.
Student: That's what I thought. But getting back to checks, why are bank drafts sometimes preferred over checks?
Cashier: Well, in the case of a check, the party who signs it is the only one who guarantees payment. But a bank draft is issued and guaranteed by a bank.
Student: Is that true of cashier's checks, too?
Cashier: Yes. And also of certified checks and bank money orders.
Student: What about sight drafts?
Cashier: Now, sight drafts are different. They're a form of request for payment through a bank.

B. Terminology Practice

bank draft: a type of exchange; a document whereby a bank requests another bank to accept **liability** for making payment

Why are bank drafts sometimes preferred over checks?
The payment was made by bank draft.
Please give me a bank draft for this amount.

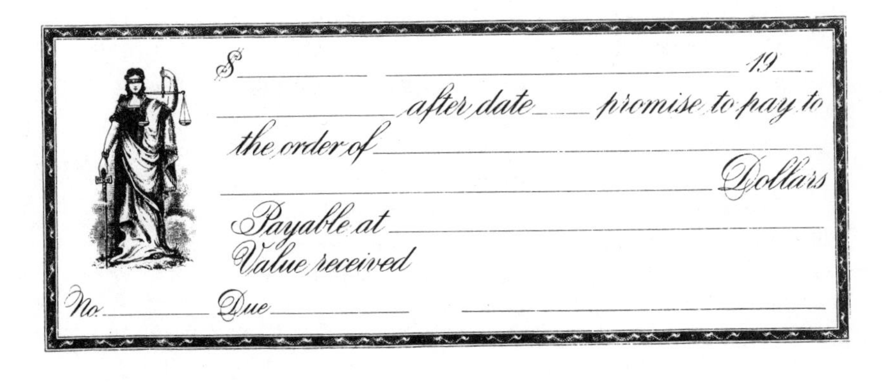

$ ____ ____ 19__
____ after date ____ promise to pay to
the order of ____
____ Dollars
Payable at ____
Value received
No. ____ Due ____ ____

PERSONAL
MONEY ORDER
THE BANK OF NEW YORK
BN1086467
NEW YORK, N.Y.
1-1
210
PAY
TO THE
ORDER OF
NOT VALID OVER $1000.
CANCELLED
Signature
NEW YORK'S FIRST BANK · FOUNDED 1784
1086467 021000018 99 6513

bank money order: a type of exchange; a bank's unqualified promise to pay a specified sum to a specific individual or corporation, sold by the bank against payment of cash.

That's also true of bank money orders.
I can give you a bank money order, if you prefer that.
He always pays us by bank money order.

TELLERS'
CHECK
THE BANK OF NEW YORK
BN 050931
NEW YORK, N.Y.
1-1
210
PAY
$
FOR
TO THE
ORDER
OF
CANCELLED
NOT VALID OVER $5,000.
AUTHORIZED SIGNATURE
NEW YORK'S FIRST BANK · FOUNDED 1784
050931 021000018 99 5738

bank note: a currency issued to a bank by the Federal Reserve Banks

Well, what's a bank note?
Are there bank notes in all denominations?
Yes, a bank note is legal tender.

bearer: the person who is named as **payee** in a piece of exchange, or who presents it for payment

The bearer need only present proper identification.
The check is made out to the bearer.
Doesn't the bearer also guarantee payment?

bill: in this sense, a piece of paper currency

We constantly handle bills of every denomination.
This bill is torn almost in half.
May I please have some small bills?

cash: change into currency

Even merchants will cash them.

They won't cash it without proper identification.

I'd like to cash this bank draft, please.

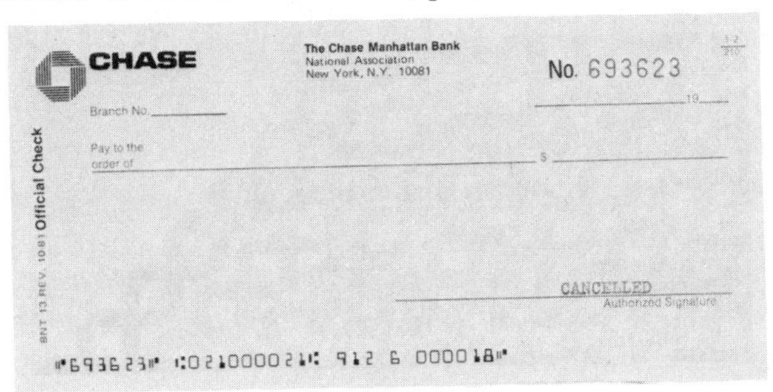

cashier's check: a negotiable form of exchange issued by a bank to a specific order and **endorsed** by an officer of the bank

Is that true of cashier's checks, too?

Do you issue many cashier's checks?

A cashier's check was enclosed with the letter.

certificate: a written statement given or held as proof of something

They're legal tender just as silver certificates are.

The certificate indicates the amount of money involved.

The president will sign the certificate.

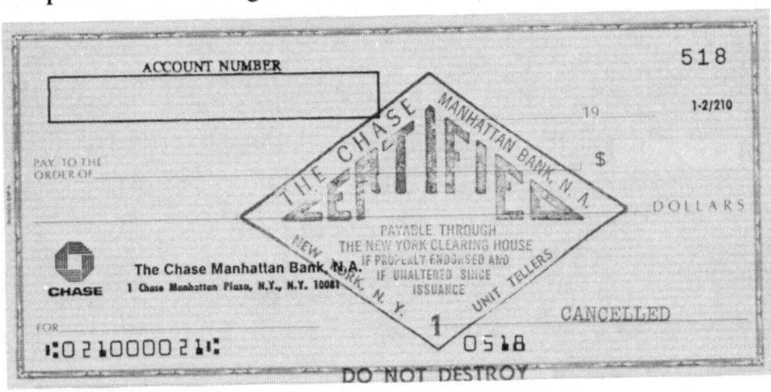

certified check: a type of exchange; a check drawn by an account holder and certified by the bank that funds are available

That's also true of certified checks.

A certified check would be safer.

Have we issued any certified checks today?

certify: guarantee the truth or worth of something
That's also true of certified checks.
The bank will certify this check.
It must be certified in writing.

check: in this sense, a written order to a bank to pay the stated amount of money
But a check isn't legal tender.
We never accept checks from strangers.
The check was cashed on the first of the month.

coin: a piece of currency made of metal
We constantly handle coins of every denomination.
This type of coin is no longer used.
These coins will have to be counted again.

currency: in this sense, money issued by the government for general use
They're what you call currency.
They'll accept payment only in currency.
What's the total amount of currency on hand?

denomination: in this sense, unit of value
We handle coins and bills of every denomination.
What denominations would you like?
The bills were in smaller denominations.

exchange: in this sense, a means of transferring money; anything with money value used in such an action
The bank must use just about every form of exchange.
Were there any fees involved in the exchange?
Currency is a form of exchange.

Federal Reserve System: a banking system set up by the government of the United States to regulate currency and banking policies

Bank notes are issued by the banks of the Federal Reserve System.
Is this bank a member of the Federal Reserve System?
The Federal Reserve System was set up in 1913.

identification: proof that a person is who he or she says he is

The bearer need only present proper identification.
Do you have some kind of identification?
Many people carry identification cards.

in lieu of: instead of

They're generally accepted in lieu of currency.
Can you give me something to hold in lieu of a certificate?
Whatever you accept in lieu of money should be negotiable.

issue: in this sense, prepare and give out

They're issued by the banks of the Federal Reserve System.
By what bank was the money order issued?
The certified check was issued just a week ago.

legal tender: money guaranteed by a government

They're what you call legal tender.
Legal tender is not always the safest form of exchange.
Gold coins aren't legal tender any more.

negotiable: able to be given over to another party

They're immediately negotiable everywhere.
Is this a negotiable form of exchange?
I'd prefer something more negotiable.

sight draft: a form of request for payment through a bank

Now, sight drafts are different.
Get the bank to present your sight draft.
We received the sight draft in this morning's mail.

CHASE
The Chase Manhattan Bank
National Association
New York, New York 10081
B666820
Date
Branch Address
Against This Check Please Pay
No Duplicate Issued
Pay to the order of
Payable at the buying rate for sight drafts on New York if issued in U.S. dollars
To
CANCELLED
BFX 137 REV 7-80
Authorized Signature
Page No.

silver certificate: a type of paper currency issued by the government against silver deposited with it

They're legal tender just as silver certificates are.

Are silver certificates issued in all denominations?

Is it a silver certificate or a bank note?

traveler's check: a check issued by a bank or other qualified corporation in a fixed denomination and becoming negotiable upon **endorsement** by the purchaser

Are traveler's checks currency?

What's the fee for issuing traveler's checks?

Would you cash some traveler's checks for me?

C. Check-Up

Fill in the blanks with the proper terms from the list.

bank draft	identification
cash	in lieu of
check	issued
currency	negotiable
denominations	sight draft

1. When I travel I don't like to carry a lot of coins and bills. I carry only small amounts of ______.
2. I carry traveler's checks, which I can change into coins and bills wherever I am. I can ______ them anywhere.
3. They can easily be given over to a third party. They're immediately ______.
4. You can buy them in different sizes or amounts. They come in different ______.
5. Many merchants won't accept a written order to your bank to pay the amount you state. They won't accept a ______.
6. This is true even if you have proof that you are who you say you are. They won't accept it even if you present proper ______.
7. Of course, people who know you will usually accept them instead of currency. They'll accept them ______ currency.
8. To settle business accounts I usually use one of the forms of exchange prepared and given out by a bank. They're ______ by a bank.
9. One type that I often use is drawn by one bank on another bank. This is called a ______.
10. To request payment of an amount due me, I often use another form of exchange presented through a bank. I use a ______.

LESSON

Checking Accounts

A. Dialogue

Clerk: Now this is the checking account ledger. Each page is a record of a customer's deposits and withdrawals.

Cashier: And you give a copy of this to the customer.

Clerk: That's right. That's his statement, which he receives with all his canceled checks. Then he reconciles it with his own records.

Cashier: This one is a joint account, isn't it? And pretty active.

Clerk: Yes, it is.

Cashier: What's this debit?

Clerk: That's our service charge.

Cashier: I notice an overdraft here in February.

Cashier: I'm afraid we've had to remind this man and his wife several times that they must keep a sufficient balance to cover all outstanding checks.

Clerk: Will I have to learn to recognize all our customers' signatures?

Cashier: Yes, you will. Any check we cash must have a genuine signature. But we keep a file of them that you can refer to.

Clerk: Will I be doing any posting of this ledger?

Cashier: Oh, yes.

B. Terminology Practice

active: in this sense, frequently used

And it's a pretty active account.
How active is their account?
This account hasn't been very active lately.

balance: in this sense, the amount remaining in an account

They must keep a sufficient balance.
Would you tell me my balance, please?
Your balance is below the minimum.

canceled: in this sense, stamped to indicate that payment has been made

He receives this with all his canceled checks.
You can use your canceled check as proof of payment.
I haven't received my canceled checks yet.

debit: *n.*, a figure in a ledger indicating a withdrawal or a charge; *v.*, to deduct from an account

What's this debit?
Total all the debits on this page.
The debit is larger than the balance.

deposit: money put into an account

Each page is a record of deposits and withdrawals.
He made his first deposit in May.
Is the deposit large enough to cover the overdraft?

genuine: true, actually being what it appears to be

Any check we cash must have a genuine signature.
Oh, I'm sure the draft is genuine.
Are you sure the certificate is genuine?

joint account: an account held in the names of two or more persons

This one is a joint account, isn't it?
We set up a joint account for them.
It's a joint account, but she seldom uses it.

ledger: a book in which records of accounts are kept

This is the checking account ledger.
Nothing like that is shown on the ledger.
One of my jobs is to keep this ledger up to date.

outstanding: in this sense, written but not yet presented for payment by the bank

The balance must cover all outstanding checks.
I have two outstanding checks for $50.00 each.
What's the total of your outstanding checks?

overdraft: an amount by which withdrawals are greater than the balance in an account

I notice an overdraft here in February.
The bank called to say that I have an overdraft.
I'm awfully embarrassed about this overdraft.

posting: in this sense, recording figures in a ledger

Will I be doing any posting of this ledger?
The posting isn't finished yet.
Most of my work is posting.

reconcile: in this sense, compare and make agree

He reconciles it with his own records.
You should reconcile your account every month.
When I reconciled my account, I found the mistake.

service charge: in this sense, a fee collected by a bank for its checking account services

That's our service charge.
How do you figure your service charge?
There's no service charge on this account

signature: a person's name as he or she writes it

Will I have to learn to recognize all our customers' signatures?
Are you sure the signature is genuine?
Will you please sign this signature card?

statement: in this sense, a record of a customer's deposits and withdrawals

That's his statement.
We mail statements to all our customers.
I think there's a small error in my statement.

withdrawal: money removed from an account; the act of removing it
Each page is a record of deposits and withdrawals.
You made two withdrawals on this date.
The last withdrawal has not been subtracted from the balance.

C. Check-Up

Fill in the blanks with the proper terms from the list.

balance	overdraft
canceled	reconciled
deposits	service charge
joint account	statement
outstanding	withdrawals

1. My wife and I have a checking account in both our names. We have a ______.
2. We both work and both put money into the account. We both make ______.
3. But we sometimes get mixed up about the amounts of money we've removed from the account. We get confused about our ______.
4. Once or twice the amount remaining in the account has gotten too low. We've had too small a ______.
5. That caused us to write a check for more money than the balance in the account. We had an ______.
6. The only way we could straighten out the account was to get a record of our deposits and withdrawals from the bank. We got a ______.
7. Of course, we also got the checks which had been stamped to indicate that payment had been made. We got our ______ checks.
8. Then we added up the checks that had been written but had not yet been paid by the bank. We totaled our ______ checks.
9. We also subtracted from our balance the bank's fee for their services. We subtracted the ______.
10. Finally, we made our records agree with the statement. We ______ our account.

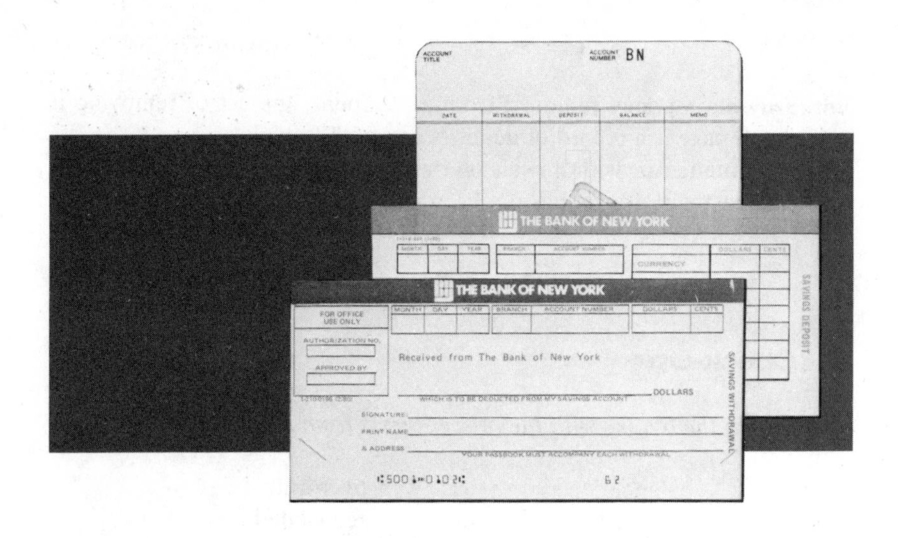

LESSON

Time Deposits, Savings Accounts, and NOW Accounts

A. Dialogue

Investor: I have some funds on hand, and I'm wondering whether I ought to put them in a savings account.

Banker: That's one possibility. A savings account is fairly liquid, although as many as 30 days notice of withdrawal may be required. A more liquid investment that also pays interest is the Negotiable Order of Withdrawal, known as the NOW account. NOW accounts have become very popular lately.

Investor: Why is that?

Banker: They have an advantage over regular checking accounts in that they pay interest, and they're more liquid than savings accounts since you can draw checks on them.

Investor: How does a time deposit differ from a savings deposit?

Banker: Well, a time deposit is for a specified term, whereas you can make withdrawals from a savings account at any time; although, as I said before, as many as 30 days notice of withdrawal may be required. A time deposit also offers a higher rate of interest than a savings deposit. This is partially due to its fixed maturity.

Investor: How do you compute the interest on a savings account?
Banker: It's compounded and credited to the account quarterly.
Investor: You mean added to the principal?
Banker: Yes. And we issue you a passbook on your savings account in which each deposit and withdrawal is entered.
Investor: Is either type of account transferable?
Banker: Only time certificates.
Investor: Are time and savings deposits insured?
Banker: Yes. We're a member of the Federal Deposit Insurance Corporation (FDIC), which insures accounts up to $40,000. Although most banks are members of the FDIC, membership is not compulsory for state-regulated banks.

B. Terminology Practice

compound: in this sense, figure interest on the principal plus any accrued interest

It's compounded and added to the account.
You'll have to learn how to compound interest.
Have you compounded the interest on that account?

credit: in this sense, add to an account; enter in a ledger so that the balance is increased

It's compounded and credited to the account.
Can you credit my account with that amount?
I don't think the deposit was credited to my account.

Federal Deposit Insurance Corporation (FDIC): an agency of the government of the United States that insures up to $40,000 of the account of each depositor in state and national banks

We're a member of the FDIC.
When was the FDIC established?
Every national bank must belong to the FDIC.

funds: money

I have some idle funds.
They don't have the necessary funds.
His funds are low at this time.

insurance: protection against a loss

We're a member of the FDIC.

Insurance usually doesn't cover the entire loss.

How much insurance do you have on your car?

liquid: in this sense, readily changeable into money

You should keep your investment fairly liquid.

Liquid investments usually yield less.

Is this type of investment liquid?

maturity: in this sense, the point at which a loan or investment is due

We pay the maximum four percent per annum at maturity.

What is the maturity date for this loan?

The interest is payable only at maturity.

Negotiable Order of Withdrawal (NOW) account: interest-bearing checking account

I put $300 in a NOW account.

I prefer NOW accounts to savings accounts.

Can I open a NOW account at this bank?

notice: in this sense, an announcement

Thirty days' notice of withdrawal may be required.

I received a notice that my loan is due.

We mail the notices ahead of time.

passbook: a small book issued to a savings account customer in which each deposit and withdrawal is entered

We issue you a passbook on your savings account.

You can't make a withdrawal without your passbook, so remember to bring it with you.

Keep your passbook in a safe place.

principal: in this sense, the unpaid balance or portion of a loan or investment, on which the interest is figured

Interest is added to the principal.

Are you making payments on the principal?

This is the original amount of the principal.

quarterly: four times a year

Interest was payed quarterly.

Quarterly payments were made on this account.

Are the payments made quarterly?

rate of interest: the percentage paid for the use of money

Do these accounts draw the same rate of interest?

Interest accrues at the rate of three percent.

The maximum rate of interest set by law is six percent per annum.

term: in this sense, a period of time
Your time deposit is for a specific term.
I'm interested in making a long-term investment.
Does this bank offer short-term loans?

time certificate: a certificate given to one who makes a time deposit
We pay four percent on a one-year time certificate.
Your time certificate is proof of your deposit.
The time certificate shows the date of maturity.

time deposit: a savings deposit made for a specified term
You might also consider a time deposit.
My time deposit draws four percent interest.
The interest is higher on a time deposit.

transferable: able to be signed over to another person
Is either type of account transferable?
I'd rather have my money in a transferable account.
When he bought it, he understood that it was transferable.

C. Check-Up

Fill in the blanks with the proper terms for the list.

FDIC	credited
compounded	rate of interest
maturity	term
NOW	time deposit
principal	liquid

1. The balance of a loan or investment is called the ______.
2. The account which resembles a checking account but pays interest is called a __________ account.
3. In some types of accounts, interest is figured on the principal plus any interest that has built up. It's __________.
4. Then it's added to the account. It's __________ to the account.
5. The __________ insures accounts of depositors.
6. I have another type of account in which I have made a deposit for a specified period of time. I've agreed to leave the money on deposit for a specified __________.
7. This is called a __________.
8. The payment for its use is payable only when the investment is due. It's payable only at __________.
9. Yesterday I deposited $1,000 in a savings account. In one year I will earn $130 on this investment. The __________ is thirteen percent.
10. It's easier to change government bonds into money than to sell a piece of land. Government bonds are more __________.

LESSON 5 Loans (1)

A. Dialogue

Banker:	Our discount committee is still discussing your application for credit. I wonder if you'd mind giving us some more information about certain items shown on your balance sheet.
Manufacturer:	Not at all.
Banker:	Is the mortgage on your fixed assets being amortized?
Manufacturer:	Yes. We're making semi-annual payments on this obligation.
Banker:	Your balance sheet shows some other indebtedness. Are any of your assets pledged as security?
Manufacturer:	No. That's just an open note.
Banker:	Would your company be willing to pledge part of its current assets as collateral security to our loan?
Manufacturer:	We wouldn't object to that. Part of this money will be used to retire present debts and part to expand our operations. Then we can immediately begin to liquidate this new liability.
Banker:	I think we'd prefer that arrangement.

B. Terminology Practice

amortize: make regular payments on the principal as well as the interest

Is the mortgage on your fixed assets being amortized?

We'd like this indebtedness to be amortized.

At what rate can you amortize this note?

asset: anything owned that has financial value

Is the mortgage on your fixed assets being amortized?

The balance in your savings account is an asset.

Then subtract your liabilities from your assets.

balance sheet: a brief statement of a party's financial condition

We want more information about certain items on your balance sheet.

You should first prepare a balance sheet.

List all your assets on the balance sheet.

collateral: anything pledged as security for a loan

Would your company pledge part of its current assets as collateral security?

What can you offer as collateral?

I'm afraid we'd require more collateral security.

credit: in this sense, permission to borrow money as the need arises

They're still discussing your application for credit.

We'll be glad to extend credit to your company.

That's a credit account, isn't it?

current assets: assets other than **real estate**, which can be readily changed into money

Would your company pledge part of its current assets?

What does he have in the way of current assets?

Their current assets will be sufficient collateral.

debt: anything owed

Part of this money will be used to retire present debts.

He's extremely worried about his debts.

Our profits will be used to pay off our debt.

discount: in this sense, having to do with making loans and purchasing investments at a price below their maturity value so that a profit can be made

Our discount committee is still discussing your application.

The discount department will have to handle this matter.

When will the discount committee meet?

fixed asset: an asset, such as real estate which cannot be readily changed into money

Is the mortgage on your fixed assets being amortized?
His fixed assets include an apartment house.
What is the total value of your fixed assets?

indebtedness: debt

Your balance sheet shows some other indebtedness.
I want to liquidate my indebtedness.
Indebtedness is a liability.

liability: in this sense, any financial obligation

We can begin to liquidate this new liability.
Are these your only liabilities?
We want to clean up some of our liabilities.

liquidate: in this sense, pay off

We can begin to liquidate this new liability.
They've asked me to liquidate the note soon.
He's liquidated all his liabilities.

mortgage: an agreement to give up the collateral which has been pledged if a debt is not paid

Is the mortgage on your fixed assets being amortized?
Do you have a mortgage on this building?
What's the term of the mortgage?

note: in this sense, an agreement between a borrower and a lender; the written promise to repay a loan

That's just an open note.
We hold his note for $1,000.
When does the note fall due?

obligation: in this sense, an indebtedness one must repay

We're making semi-annual payments on this obligation.
Do you have any other obligations to meet this month?
Those are the only obligations I have.

open note: a note, the payment of which is not guaranteed by collateral security

That's just an open note.
Shall we let him have the money on an open note?
I wouldn't take his open note for that large an amount.

pledge: in this sense, promise as security

Are any of your assets pledged as security?
I think he'd pledge his fixed assets.
All their current assets have been pledged on another loan.

retire: in this sense, pay off

Part of this money will be used to retire present debts.
When will you be able to retire this indebtedness?
We can't discuss another loan until this one has been retired.

security: in this sense, a guarantee of payment

Are any of your assets pledged as security?
What kind of security can you put up?
The committee feels that this isn't enough security.

C. Check-Up

Fill in the blanks with the proper terms from the list.

amortized	collateral
balance sheet	credit
fixed assets	current assets
liquidate	open note
mortgage	pledge

1. I went to the bank this week to apply for permission to borrow money as the need arises. I applied for ______.
2. They asked me for a brief statement of my financial condition. They wanted a ______.
3. I'd hoped I wouldn't have to put up security for a loan. I'd hoped to get the money on an ______.
4. However, they wanted me to offer some of my assets which can be readily changed into money as security. They wanted me to offer some of my ______.
5. They wanted some ______ security.
6. They wanted me to ______ some of these assets.
7. There are already obligations against my real estate. There are obligations against my ______.
8. They wanted me to make an agreement to give up my assets if the loan isn't paid. They wanted me to give them a ______.
9. I agreed to do this and to pay off some of the principal each year along with the interest. The amount I owe will be ______.
10. I expect to pay off this indebtedness in five years. I'll ______ it in that time.

LESSON

Loans (2)

A. Dialogue

Builder: I received your notice that my note is due. I can pay it off now, but there's a piece of land right next to my property that I'd like to buy.

Banker: I don't remember your situation exactly. Are your present holdings free of encumbrance?

Builder: My real estate is clear. But there's a chattel mortgage on my construction equipment.

Banker: Has this land you want to buy been appraised?

Builder: Yes. It belongs to an estate and was appraised by order of the court. They estimated its value at $10,500.

Banker: Can it be bought for that figure?

Builder: I think so. I'd like to make them that offer.

Banker: Would you consider giving us a trust deed to secure your present note plus the additional funds you'll need?

Builder: I might. But I'd thought that my net worth is high enough that I could borrow the amount on my open note.

Banker: Well, in that case, would your wife agree to be a co-signer?

Builder: I'm sure she would, because title to the property will be in both our names.

Banker: Well, it seems to me that you have enough equity in your property for us to make the loan on an open note.

B. Terminology Practice

appraise: judge the value of

It was appraised by order of the court.
Has someone been appointed to appraise the property?
The land was appraised at $8,000.

chattel: any personal or movable possession, such as furniture or equipment

There's a chattel mortgage on my construction equipment.
Your automobile is a chattel.
A house is not a chattel.

chattel mortgage: a mortgage on chattels

There's a chattel mortgage on my construction equipment.
We took a chattel mortgage on his livestock.
I want to liquidate my chattel mortgage.

clear: in this sense, without encumbrance

My real estate is clear.
In six months all my property will be clear.
His balance sheet shows that he's clear of indebtedness.

co-signer: a person who signs a document with another person and shares the obligation

Would your wife agree to be a co-signer?
His partner will be the co-signer.
Can you get someone to be your co-signer?

deed: in this sense, a document which proves a change of ownership of real estate

Would you consider giving us a trust deed?
Who holds the deed to the property?
The deed must be signed by both parties.

encumbrance: in this sense, an indebtedness, such as a mortgage

Are your present holdings free of encumbrance?

There's no encumbrance on his real estate.

The encumbrance isn't large, I believe.

equity: in this sense, the value of a piece of property beyond any indebtedness held against it

It seems to me that you have enough equity in your property.

He must have quite a lot of equity in it, by now.

Your equity grows each time you make a payment on the indebtedness.

estate: in this sense, the holdings and obligations left by a dead person

It belongs to an estate.

Our bank will administer the estate.

How large an estate did he leave?

estimate: judge the value of

They estimated its value at $10,500.

I wouldn't estimate his holdings that high.

What do you estimate the loss will be?

holding: something owned, such as property or **securities**

Are your present holdings clear of encumbrance?

He's greatly increased his holdings over the years.

Are most of your holdings in real estate?

net: in this sense, the amount remaining after all expenses or obligations have been subtracted

I'd thought that my net worth is high enough.

What are your net earnings?

This figure is our net profits for the year.

net worth: the value of one's holdings after all obligations have been subtracted

I'd thought that my net worth is high enough.

He gave us a statement showing his net worth.

What would you estimate their net worth to be?

property: in this sense, anything owned, especially real estate or land

There's a piece of land right next to my property.

Doesn't your property border on his?

What's the total value of your property?

real estate: land, including anything constructed on it

My real estate is clear.

I think she holds quite a lot of real estate.

He makes his living by selling real estate.

secure: *v.*, in this sense, to guarantee payment of
Would you give us a trust deed to secure the funds you'll need?
What's the loan secured by?
I'd rather see the loan secured by some fixed assets.

title: in this sense, the record or proof of ownership of property
Title to the property will be in both our names.
Will the bank hold title to the property?
In whose name is the title held?

trust: in this sense, the legal responsibility given to one party to act for another in financial matters
Would you consider giving us a trust deed?
This money is to be held in trust for his daughter.
Most of my work is with trusts.

trust deed: a deed to real estate held as security for a loan—in effect, a mortgage
Would you consider giving us a trust deed?
Please come in to sign the trust deed.
Our lawyer will prepare a trust deed.

C. Check-Up

Fill in the blanks with the proper terms from the list.

appraised	holdings
chattel mortgage	net worth
clear	real estate
co-signer	secure
encumbrance	trust deed

1. All the things I own are free from mortgage or any other indebtedness. All my ______ are without indebtedness.
2. They're ______.
3. They're free from ______.
4. I want to buy some land which has a house on it. I want to buy some ______.
5. I've applied for a loan, and I think the total value of my possessions is high enough for me to borrow the money on an open note. I think my ______ is high enough for that.

6. But the bank wants me to put up some of my property to guarantee payment. They want me to do this to ______ the loan.
7. They want me to give them a mortgage on my furniture and other movable possessions. They want a ______.
8. Or they want me to give a deed to the property which will be held as security to the loan. They want a ______.
9. In either case, they want my wife to sign with me and share the obligation. They want her to be a ______.
10. The property I'm buying has been judged to be worth $9,300. It's been ______ at that amount.

LESSON

7 Bank Investments

A. Dialogue

Board Member: I notice that our cash and cash-in-banks has been building up above the amount required by law. Do you think we could invest some of these excess reserves profitably?

President: I've had the same thought. And right now there's a new offering of municipal bonds that can be bought at a price that will yield ten percent. On the other hand, the variance of demand deposits seems to be rising, and we don't want to be caught in a position where we have to borrow reserves.

Board Member: That's a good point. We should certainly maintain some excess reserves. Are the municipal bonds general obligation bonds?

President: Yes, they are. I prefer those to revenue bonds, don't you?

Board Member: Yes, I do. Does this issue have an AA rating?

President: Yes. And these bonds can mature in either five or ten years. They're tax-exempt, you know.

Board Member: Do you think we might also buy some stocks to keep our portfolio well diversified?

President: Well, we might. We might also consider buying some Swiss francs. The problem with both of these, however, is that they tend to be much more speculative than bonds. Because of our low equity/deposit ratio we can't afford to buy very volatile assets.

Board Member: Unless we stick to blue chip issues. They show less price fluctuation.

B. Terminology Practice

AA rating: a high estimate of the value of a bond or stock, the ratings are made impartially by a company whose specialty is evaluation of investments

Does this issue have an AA rating?
These bonds are given an AA rating.
I prefer to buy something of AA rating.

blue chip: a stock thought to be of highest quality

We can stick to blue chip issues.
Is there a new offering of blue chip stocks?
Their portfolio is made up entirely of blue chip stocks.

bond: in this sense, a unit of fixed obligation of a company or government for a fixed term

There's a new offering of municipal bonds.
What rate of interest do those bonds pay?
Bonds are transferable, aren't they?

cash: coins and bills

I notice that our cash has been building up.
How much cash do we have on hand?
Many merchants will only sell for cash.

cash-in-banks: cash kept in other banks as a reserve
    I notice that our cash-in-banks has been building up.
    Isn't our cash-in-banks pretty low?
    We can make a withdrawal from our cash-in-banks.

diversified: in this sense, made up of a variety of stocks and bonds
    Shouldn't we keep our portfolio well diversified?
    Our bank's assets are well diversified.
    It's desirable to diversify your investments.

equity/deposit ratio: total assets minus total liabilities divided by deposits
    A high equity/deposit ratio serves as a cushion against hard times.
    Does a high equity/deposit ratio protect the depositor?
    Most banks have low equity/deposit ratios.

excess reserves: reserves in excess of the legal requirement against bank liabilities
    Our bank has excess reserves.
    Do excess reserves rise when interest rates fall?
    Excess reserves tend to fall when the variance of demand deposits goes down.

fluctuation: a changing back and forth
    They show less price fluctuation.
    There's been a lot of fluctuation in the price.
    Some stocks show more fluctuation than others.

general obligation bond: a bond secured by all the property of a city or other unit of government
    Are they general obligation bonds?
    This is an issue of general obligation bonds.
    General obligation bonds usually pay about three percent.

issue: in this sense, all the stocks or bonds offered for sale at one time by a particular company or government
    Does this issue have an AA rating?
    Most of the issue was sold the first day.
    I wish I'd purchased some of that issue.

municipal bond: a bond offered for sale by a city or other unit of government
    There's a new offering of municipal bonds.
    What interest do these municipal bonds pay?
    Much of his portfolio is in municipal bonds.

offering: in this sense, a quantity of stocks or bonds offered for sale at one time

There's a new offering of municipal bonds.
There are some good buys in this offering.
When does the offering go on sale?

portfolio: in this sense, a list of stocks and bonds belonging to one holder

Shouldn't we keep our portfolio well diversified?
I want to add some revenue bonds to my portfolio.
She's learned to manage her portfolio herself.

revenue: in this sense, money earned by a government especially for the performance of a public service

I prefer those to revenue bonds, don't you?
This service brings in a lot of revenue.
How much revenue does the water company earn?

revenue bond: a bond which is repaid out of revenues

I prefer those to revenue bonds, don't you?
The city is issuing some revenue bonds.
The company is selling its revenue bonds.

speculative: in this sense, bought and sold in an attempt to make profits from price fluctuations

But stocks are so much more speculative.
I don't like to take a chance on speculative stocks.
He's made a lot of money from speculative buying and selling.

stock: in this sense, a unit of ownership in a company

Do you think we might also buy some stocks?
These stocks should pay a good profit.
The value of these stocks has risen sharply.

tax: money collected by a government for its support

What is the sales tax in New Jersey?
I hear that the tax rate will be increased.
Have you figured in the tax?

tax-exempt: free from tax obligation

They're tax-exempt, you know.
What kinds of bonds are tax-exempt?
The government encourages sale of these bonds by making them tax-exempt.

variance of demand deposits: the degree of fluctuation in the inflows and outflows of demand deposits (checking accounts)

The bank's variance of deposits has increased lately.
Banks estimate expected variance of deposits.
High variance of deposits can reduce potential bank profits.

yield: in this sense, earn

They can be bought at a price that will yield three and a half percent.
This investment doesn't yield very much.
What did these stocks yield last year?

C. Check-Up

Fill in the blanks with the proper terms from the list.

bonds	revenue bonds
diversified	speculative
fluctuation	stocks
issue	tax-exempt
portfolio	yield

1. I want to make an investment, and I've been thinking of buying some units of ownership in a company. I may buy some ______.
2. I don't want an investment that does a lot of changing back and forth in price. I'm not interested in anything that has a lot of price ______.
3. I'm willing to let other people try to make profits by buying and selling investments of this kind. I'll let them make the ______ investments.
4. I may also buy some units of fixed obligation of a company or government for a fixed term. I may buy some ______.
5. I'll add these to my list of such investments. I'll add them to my ______.
6. I like to have a variety of investments on my list. I like it to be ______.
7. My city is offering some of these for sale right now. They're putting an ______ on sale.
8. They're the type that will be repaid out of the earnings from a public service. They're ______.
9. I won't have to pay any tax on them. They're ______.
10. They earn three and a half percent interest. They ______ three and a half percent.

LESSON

Types of Banking Institutions

A. Dialogue

Student: What type of bank is this?
Banker: We're a commercial bank.
Student: Does that mean that your services are limited?
Banker: To some extent. For instance, we can't offer the fiduciary services that a trust company can.
Student: What are they?
Banker: Well, they have to do with the administration of trusts and estates.
Student: Suppose I wanted to buy or sell some securities. Does your bank handle such transactions?
Banker: Yes, through our brokerage house.
Student: Is your broker a member of the stock exchange?
Banker: Yes.
Student: This is a state bank, isn't it?
Banker: That's right.

Student: Do you offer fewer services than a national bank?
Banker: No. In general, the only difference is that a state bank gets its charter from the state it's in, and the national bank gets its charter from the federal government in Washington, D.C.
Student: Are there banks that don't offer regular commercial services?
Banker: Oh, yes. For example, savings and loan associations and the federal land banks are only lending institutions.
Student: Would you say a savings and loan association is a bank?
Banker: No. I'd rather call it a financial institution.
Student: How about a credit union?
Banker: That's not really a bank, either. In general, commercial banks differ from these other financial intermediaries in the degree and form of regulation they are subject to. With the general decline in regulation over the past five years, commercial banks are becoming more and more like other financial intermediaries. For instance, federally chartered credit unions can now offer checkable deposits.
Student: Do you mean NOW accounts?
Banker: Not exactly. They're called draft accounts, but they're similar to NOW accounts.

B. Terminology Practice

broker: a person who sells or buys stocks and bonds for others
Is your broker a member of the stock exchange?
I'll get in touch with my broker about this.
What kind of fee do you pay your broker?

brokerage: the buying and selling of stocks and bonds for other persons
We handle such transactions through our brokerage house.
The brokerage fee won't be very large.
They're discussing some brokerage transactions.

brokerage house: an institution which handles brokerage
We handle such transactions through our brokerage house.
We received the information from our brokerage house.
My brokerage house says these stocks have an AA rating.

commercial bank: a bank whose major services are accepting and protecting money for deposit and paying checks issued by the depositors; laws permit it to invest for profit a portion of this money

Where is the local commercial bank?

They're trying to get a charter for a commercial bank.

He's had years of commercial bank experience.

credit union: an institution formed by a group of persons who combine their savings in order to make loans to members at a low rate of interest

How about a credit union?

You must join a credit union before you borrow from it.

Does your company have a credit union?

exchange: in this sense, a place where business transactions are made

Is your broker a member of the stock exchange?

The farmers have set up an exchange.

The exchange has been very successful, hasn't it?

federal land bank: a bank established by the government of the United States to make loans for the purchase of land

The federal land banks are only lending institutions.

The loan was made by a federal land bank.

How many federal land banks are there?

fiduciary: having to do with a truust

We can't offer fiduciary services.

I want to discuss some fiduciary matters with them.

He'll turn it over to some fiduciary institution.

financial intermediary: a financial institution that acts as a middleman, transferring funds from ultimate lenders to ultimate borrowers

Commercial banks are the financial intermediaries with the largest asset size.

Composition of assets and liabilities differs significantly from one type of financial intermediary to another.

Commercial banks are the most widely diversified of all financial intermediaries in terms of both their assets and liabilities.

lending: in this sense, empowered to make loans

These banks are only lending institutions.

Their lending powers are limited by law.

They've had to change their lending policies.

national bank: a bank which has a charter from the federal government

Do you offer fewer services than a national bank?

Are there more national banks than state banks?

I believe he's employed in a national bank.

savings and loan association: an institution which accepts savings deposits and makes loans mainly for the purchase and repair of homes

Would you say a savings and loan association is a bank?

I hope to get a loan from the savings and loan association.

The interest on deposits is usually higher in a savings and loan association.

security: in this sense, a stock or bond

Suppose I wanted to buy or sell some securities.

These are all blue chip securities.

Securities are transferable, aren't they?

state bank: a bank which has a charter from a state government

This is a state bank, isn't it?

Your deposits are just as safe in a state bank.

All the state banks have received this notice.

stock exchange: a place where stocks are bought and sold

Is your broker a member of the stock exchange?

Was there much activity on the stock exchange today?

Not all stock transactions go through the stock exchange.

transaction: a business action

Does your bank handle such transactions?

Were you a party to the transaction?

The transaction was definitely not legal.

trust company: an institution which manages trusts and estates

We can't offer the services that a trust company can.

Which trust company is managing the estate?

Does a trust company have to have a charter?

C. Check-Up

Fill in the blanks with the proper terms from the list.

brokerage house	lending
commercial banks	national bank
credit union	savings and loan association
federal land bank	securities
fiduciary	trust company

1. In our city there are a number of institutions which make loans. There are numerous ______ institutions.
2. You can borrow money from the ______, although their major service is checking accounts.
3. The one I bank with has a charter from the federal government. It's a ______.
4. There's also a bank established by the federal government to make loans for the purchase of land. It's called a ______.
5. Then you can borrow money for the purchase or repair of your home, as well as make savings deposits, at a ______.
6. Many of the people who work at my company belong to the ______, which they formed by combining their savings in order to make loans to members at a low rate of interest.
7. If you have problems that have to do with trusts or estates, you take them to a ______.
8. They handle ______ matters.
9. And if you want to buy or sell some stocks, you go to a ______.
10. They handle ______.

LESSON

Trust Services

A. Dialogue

Banker: Mrs. Powers, I was very sorry to hear of your husband's death.
Client: Thank you. I'm pleased that the bank was named executor of the estate.
Banker: We'll help you in every way we can. We've looked through the contents of the safe-deposit box and made an inventory. Everything seems to be in good order.
Client: I'm most concerned about my immediate living expenses.
Banker: Well, we're empowered under the terms of the will to provide you with an allowance until the estate has been probated.
Client: Oh, that's fine.
Banker: And there are three life insurance policies. You're the beneficiary in each of them.
Client: Yes, I knew about those.

Banker: The benefits from these policies will be paid directly to you within the next two weeks.

Client: Excellent.

Banker: The income from your inheritance is going to be quite sizable. Of course, we don't know yet what demands will be made against the estate.

Client: As far as I know, there are no large creditors.

Banker: We hope not. You understand, also, that this bank is named trustee under the will. This means that we will take care of the portfolio of securities and give an annual report of all transactions.

Client: Yes, I understand that. Thank you for your counseling.

B. Terminology Practice

allowance: in this sense, an amount of money regularly given to a person for current expenses

We're empowered to provide you with an allowance.
Her allowance will be mailed on the first of the month.
Could the amount of the allowance be increased?

beneficiary: the party to whom property or a sum of money is given under the terms of a will or trust

You're the beneficiary in each of them.
In this estate, you are named a beneficiary.
Several beneficiaries were named in the will.

benefits: in this sense, payments

The benefits will be paid directly to you.
What benefits may I expect from the trust?
Will these benefits be tax-exempt?

counseling: having to do with giving advice

Our counseling service is for people in just your position.
May we offer you our counseling services?
They'll probably need some counseling.

creditor: a party to whom a debt is owed

There are no large creditors.
His creditors are requesting payment.
You have a letter from a creditor.

demand: in this sense, a request for payment
We don't know what demands will be made.
This note is payable on demand.
There are numerous demands against the estate.

empower: give power to
We're empowered to provide you with an allowance.
The court empowered us to collect the debt.
We are not empowered to sell any of the holdings.

executor: a party appointed to carry out the requests in a will
The bank was named executor of the estate.
Do you know who the executor is?
You must present your demand to the executor.

income: earnings
The income is going to be quite sizable.
What is the income from the investments?
Part of his income is tax-exempt.

inheritance: money or property received from an estate
The income from your inheritance is sizable.
He invested his inheritance in securities.
His inheritance consisted mostly of real estate.

inventory: a list of items of property
We've made an inventory.
Should this be listed in the inventory?
The inventory shows a large savings account.

life insurance: a sum of money payable in case of loss of life
There are three life insurance policies.
Did he have any life insurance?
Life insurance is a good investment.

policy: in this sense, an insurance contract; a certificate of such a contract
There are three life insurance policies.
She is the beneficiary of his insurance policy.
He wants to take out another life insurance policy.

probate: prove (a will) genuine and place on the records of the proper court
You'll receive an allowance until the estate has been probated.
We're empowered to probate the will.
When will it be probated?

safe-deposit box: a locked box for important papers, usually kept in a bank

We've looked through the safe-deposit box.
She says it's in the safe-deposit box.
Rent is due on your safe-deposit box.

terms: in this sense, stated conditions, as in a will or contract.
We're empowered to do this under the terms of the will.
You must obey the terms of the contract.
The terms of the will were not clear.

trustee: a party to whom a trust is given
This bank is named trustee under the will.
The trustees will meet tomorrow.
His son is the trustee of the estate.

will: a document which states how a person wishes his estate to be divided, made public only after his death
We have this power under the terms of the will.
The will must be probated in this county.
His will was written by his attorney.

C. Check-Up

Fill in the blanks with the proper terms from the list.

allowance	inheritance
beneficiary	inventory
creditors	probated
demands	safe-deposit box
executor	will

1. Mr. Carson died recently and left a document stating how he wished his estate to be divided. He left a ______.
2. It named our bank as the party who would carry out these requests. We were named the ______.
3. First, we opened the locked box where he kept his important papers. We opened the ______.
4. We made a list of the items of property he held. We made an ______.
5. We didn't know at that time whether there were any parties to whom he owed debts. We didn't know whether there were any ______.

6. We didn't know what requests for payment might be made. We didn't know what ______ might be made.
7. Mrs. Carson was named the person who would receive the money and property in the estate. She was the ______.
8. She received quite a lot of money and property. Her ______ was sizable.
9. However, she would not receive it until the will had been proved genuine and placed on the records of the court. She had to wait until the estate was ______.
10. In the meantime, we were empowered to give her an amount of money regularly for current expenses. We gave her an ______.

LESSON

LESSON 10 Brokerage Services

A. Dialogue

Customer: I have some corporate bonds that'll mature next month. Can you help me present them for redemption?

Banker: Surely. Where are they payable?

Customer: At one of the banks in New York.

Banker: Are they the registered or the coupon type?

Customer: They're registered in the names of both me and my wife.

Banker: You'll both have to assign them.

Customer: Yes, I know. And when the proceeds have come in, could you help me reinvest the funds in some preferred stocks?

Banker: Oh, yes. Our brokerage house can bid on some shares for you.

Customer: They charge the usual broker's commission, I suppose.

Banker: Yes, they charge the same as any reliable house. They have a seat on both the New York and the American Exchanges.

Customer: I've also thought of taking a flier on some common stocks, if I could find a good growth industry.

Banker: Well, the market looks favorable right now.

B. Terminology Practice

assign: in this sense, transfer ownership

You'll both have to assign them.
He has assigned the bonds to her.
To whom were they assigned?

bid: in this sense, make an offer to buy at a certain price

They can bid on some shares for you.
Would you be willing to bid a little higher?
The brokers have been bidding actively on this stock.

commission: in this sense, a charge for services in a sale, based on the amount of the transaction

They charge the usual broker's commission.
Their commission will be figured in the sale price.
He receives both salary and commission.

common stock: ordinary stock, with no fixed dividend rate

I've thought of taking a flier on some common stocks.
They've announced an issue of common stock.
You have fewer rights with common stock.

corporate bond: a bond issued by a corporation, or group of people who have a charter to act as an individual

I have some corporate bonds that'll mature next month.
Does a corporate bond pay about the same interest?
The portfolio contains mostly corporate bonds.

coupon: in this sense, a removable printed statement on a bond of the interest due at a particular time—it must be presented for collection

Are they the registered or the coupon type?
Don't forget to clip the coupons and send them in on time.
What happens if I lose a coupon?

flier: in this sense, a speculative transaction

I've thought of taking a flier on some common stocks.

He likes to take a flier on the stock market once in a while.

They've decided to take a flier on this stock.

growth: in this sense, giving promise of development, so that the value of an investment will increase

I want to find a good growth industry.

Part of your portfolio should be in growth stocks.

It's hard to decide what the growth industries are.

market: in this sense, the buying and selling which is taking place at any one time

The market looks favorable right now.

The market value of these stocks has increased.

He thinks the market is going to go down.

mature: in this sense, become due for payment

I have some corporate bonds that'll mature next month.

When do these bonds mature?

When these bonds mature I want to buy some stocks.

preferred stock: stock on which dividends are paid before those on common stock and which gives the holder some rights to any assets that are distributed

Could you help me reinvest in some preferred stocks?

He says preferred stock is a better investment.

This is an offering of preferred stocks.

proceeds: the money received from some transaction

When the proceeds come in, could you help me reinvest the funds?

The proceeds will be sizable, I believe.

What do you plan to do with the proceeds of this sale?

redemption: in this sense, the collection at maturity of money invested in a bond

Can you help me present them for redemption?

My lawyer will handle the redemption of the bonds.

I'll reinvest the proceeds from the redemption of my bonds.

registered: in this sense, having the owner's name placed on a record and on the certificate

Are they the registered or the coupon type?

They hold quite a portfolio of registered bonds.

Most of her inheritance was in registered bonds.

seat: in this sense, the right to take part as a member
They have a seat on the American Exchange.
I suppose a seat on the exchange costs a lot of money.
They lost their seat because of bad business practices.

share: in this sense, a unit of ownership in a company
They can bid on some shares for you.
How many shares do you want to buy?
Each share gives the holder one vote.

C. Check-Up

Fill in the blanks with the proper terms from the list.

bid	market
commission	preferred stocks
common stocks	proceeds
flier	redemption
growth	shares

1. I want to buy some units of ownership in a company. I want to buy some ______ of stock.
2. I'll ask my broker to make an offer of a sum of money for them. He'll ______ on them.
3. Of course, he'll make a charge for his services. He'll charge a ______.
4. The buying and selling right now are such that this looks like a good time to buy. The ______ is favorable.
5. I'd like to buy some stocks in a company that seems to be developing so that the value of my investment will increase. I'd like to buy some ______ stocks.
6. However, I'm not much interested in speculative transactions. I seldom take a ______.
7. I'd rather buy into some safe, well-established company. And I want to buy the kind of stock that pays dividends before those of the ordinary type, and the kind that gives me some rights to any assets that may be distributed. I want to buy some ______.
8. I'd rather buy these than the ordinary kind with no fixed dividend rate. I'd rather buy these than ______.
9. But first I have to collect the money I have invested in some bonds, when they mature. At that time I'll present them for ______.
10. With the money I receive from this transaction, I'll buy the stocks. I'll invest the ______ in stocks.

LESSON

11 Interbank Relations

A. Dialogue

Banker 1: How many correspondent bank accounts do you have?

Banker 2: We have reserves in six banks. Two of the accounts are inactive.

Banker 1: Do you use any clearinghouse other than the Federal Reserve Bank?

Banker 2: Yes, we also get a daily letter from our central bank in St. Louis.

Banker 1: Are you allowed to make a collection charge on your items from your central bank?

Banker 2: No. We've agreed to clear them at par.

Banker 1: Will your correspondent banks purchase any installment loans that you're not licensed to handle?

Banker 2: Yes, any that our customers are willing to endorse to them.

Banker 1: Do they advise you on your investments, like commercial paper and short-term debentures?

Banker 2: Oh, yes. And each week our New York correspondent sends us their report on financial and economic trends, including quotations on listed and unlisted stocks.

Banker 1: And they handle your foreign exchange.

Banker 2: That's right.

B. Terminology Practice

central bank: a bank which regulates the supply of currency within an area, also serving as a clearinghouse

We get a daily letter from our central bank.
Is that the only central bank you use?
We'll forward this to our central bank.

clear: in this sense, pass through a clearinghouse

We've agreed to clear them at par.
The check should have cleared by now.
We clear most of our items through a bank in Denver.

clearinghouse: an office where banks exchange checks drawn on one another

Do you use any other clearinghouse?
Our clearinghouse is in another city.
We mail our checks to the clearinghouse.

collection: in this sense, the process of obtaining payment of an item of exchange

Are you allowed to make a collection charge?
The collection of this item will be difficult.
Has it ever been presented for collection?

commercial paper: short-term obligations of industrial companies

Do they advise you on commercial paper?
Commercial paper is a good investment.
We consider commercial paper to be a liquid asset.

correspondent bank: a bank with which another bank has regular dealings

How many correspondent bank accounts do you have?
One of our correspondent banks is in New York.
Do you carry a large daily balance with your correspondent bank?

debenture: an obligation issued by a corporation which pays interest but is often unsecured

Do they advise you on short-term debentures?

Most debentures are short-term obligations.

Aren't all debentures negotiable?

endorse: in this sense, place one's signature on the back of a document in order to transfer ownership

They'll purchase any that our customers are willing to endorse.

Both parties must endorse the check.

You must endorse it in ink.

foreign exchange: any item of exchange from another nation

And they handle your foreign exchange.

Do you make a charge for handling foreign exchange?

We have a foreign exchange department.

installment: in this sense, one of several payments on an obligation

Will your correspondent bank purchase installment loans?

The first installment will be due in 30 days.

This is the last installment.

letter: in this sense, the items of exchange presented by or to a correspondent bank for collection on a particular day

We get a daily letter from our correspondent bank.

I want to ask you about one of the items in the New York letter.

Is there anything unusual in the letter?

listed: in this sense, accepted for sale on a stock exchange

They send us quotations on listed and unlisted stocks.

Is this stock listed on the New York Exchange?

How do you buy unlisted stocks?

paper: in this sense, any written promise to pay

Do they advise you on commercial paper?

We don't deal much in that kind of paper.

This paper should be a good investment.

par: in this sense, the value printed on the face of a certificate of obligation

We've agreed to clear them at par.

What is the par value per share of this stock?

The market value may be above or below par.

quotation: in this sense, a statement of the current price

They send us quotations on listed and unlisted stocks.

What is the quotation on this stock?

Have you seen today's market quotation?

C. Check-Up

Fill in the blanks with the proper terms from the list.

central banks	endorse
clearinghouses	foreign exchange
collection	letters
commercial paper	listed
correspondent banks	quotations

1. There are several banks with which we have regular dealings. We have several ______.
2. They act as offices where our bank and others exchange checks drawn on each other. They act as ______.
3. They also regulate the supply of currency in their areas. They serve as ______.
4. Each day they send us items of exchange for which they want to obtain payment. They send us daily ______.
5. They send them for ______.
6. These banks advise us about such investments as short-term obligations of industrial companies. They advise us about ______.
7. They purchase installment loans from our customers, who transfer ownership by placing their signatures on the backs of the documents. They ______ the documents to the banks.
8. These banks handle any items of exchange from other countries that we receive. They handle our ______.
9. One of these banks sends statements of the current prices on stocks which are accepted for sale by the exchanges. They send us ______ on these stocks.
10. We call these ______ stocks.

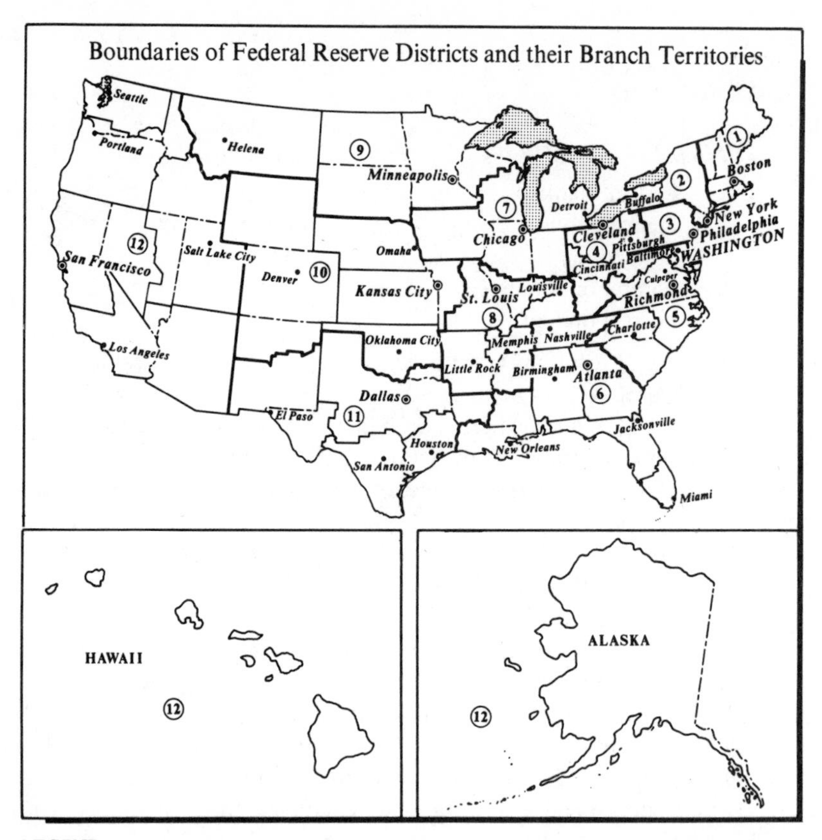

LEGEND

- Boundaries of Federal Reserve Districts
- Boundaries of Federal Reserve Branch Territories
- Board of Governors of the Federal Reserve System
- Federal Reserve Bank Cities
- Federal Reserve Branch Cities
- Federal Reserve Bank Facility

LESSON 12 The Federal Reserve System

A. Dialogue

Customer: I'm remitting by check on your bank an amount due on my note to a bank in Florida. Will that bank send the check directly to you for collection?

Banker: It could do that. But it'll probably send the check through the regular channels.

Customer: What does that mean?

Banker: Well, the bank to which your check is payable will send it to the Federal Reserve Bank (Fed) in its Reserve District for collection. The transit department of that bank will send it to the Fed in our Reserve District. From there it's sent to us. Our deposits at the Fed are reduced by the amount of the check, and the bank in Florida's reserves will rise by an equivalent amount.

Customer: So each bank in the Federal Reserve System has an account at the Federal Reserve Bank in its district?

Banker: Exactly. In this way the Federal Reserve System acts as the clearinghouse for the greater portion of the commercial banking industry.

Customer: How many Reserve Districts are there?

Banker: There are twelve, with one Reserve Bank in each district.

Customer: To become a member of the System, is a bank required to subscribe to any stock in the Reserve Bank in its district?

Banker: Yes. And, to explain further, all national banks must be members of the System. Incorporated state banks, including commercial banks, mutual savings banks, trust companies, and industrial banks, may join the System.

Customer: Other than handling items of exchange, what services do Federal Reserve Banks offer member banks?

Banker: As fiscal agents of the United States Treasury, they assist in issuing and redeeming government bonds and the refinancing of bonds that have reached maturity. They'll also accept from us any paper that can be rediscounted, if our cash reserve falls below the legal reserve requirement.

Customer: What is the legal reserve requirement?

Banker: That's the amount that banks are required to hold against their liabilities. The Money Control Act of 1980 provides that reserve requirements be uniformly applied by the Federal Reserve to all checking-type deposits at all depository institutions, regardless of Federal Reserve membership or type of institution. By 1988, all depository institutions will have to hold reserves of three percent against that portion of their checking accounts below 25 million and twelve percent against the portion above 25 million. For time and savings deposits, required reserves against individual deposits are being eliminated entirely.

Customer: How hard is it to borrow reserves from the Fed?

Banker: Banks have to meet particular requirements in order to borrow. In general, there are substantial transaction costs in the form of red tape and administrative costs. The discount rate is thus only a partial indicator of the costs involved in borrowing from the Federal Reserve Board.

B. Terminology Practice

discount rate: the interest rate that the Federal Reserve charges when it lends to member banks

The Fed often uses changes in the discount rate as an indicator of a change in policy.

The discount rate is one instrument the Fed uses to control monetary policy.

The discount rate tends to follow in the direction of other interest rates.

face value: the value printed on the bill or other instrument

The face value was less than the market value.

Were they sold at face value?

He was given a discount from face value.

fiscal: in this sense, having to do with public funds

They're fiscal agents of the United States Treasury.

There'll be some changes in fiscal policy.

He's an authority on fiscal matters.

incorporated: having a charter to act as an individual

Incorporated state banks may join the System.

Is the town incorporated?

They were incorporated in 1953.

industrial bank: a bank which makes loans for the purchase or manufacture of industrial products, using a repayment plan of certificate purchases by installment which permits higher legal rates of interest than on other loans

Industrial banks may join the System.

Have you had any dealings with industrial banks?

An industrial bank might make such a loan.

mutual: in this sense, having a structure of shared ownership by those who make use of the institution

Mutual savings banks may join the System.
Some life insurance companies have a mutual structure.
This investment company is set up on a mutual plan.

mutual savings bank: a savings bank which is owned by the depositors

Mutual savings banks may join the System.
I have an account in a mutual savings bank.
A mutual savings bank has no capital, has it?

redeem: recover ownership by paying a specified sum

When the Fed wants to ease monetary policy, it redeems government bonds.
He redeemed the stocks he had lost when he was unemployed.
Most fixed interest securities are redeemable.

rediscount: in this sense, sell (a note or other investment) at a price less than its maturity value

They'll accept any paper that can be rediscounted.
Let's see if we can't rediscount this note.
Don't you think we might rediscount some paper?

red tape: the use of official forms and procedures that impede efficiency

Governments go through a lot of red tape.
Red tape takes up too much time.
Red tape often delays transactions.

refinancing: issuing a new obligation to replace an older one

They assist in the refinancing of bonds that have reached maturity
They're interested in refinancing this piece of property.
He thinks he'll be better off by refinancing.

remit: send or pay (money)

I'm remitting my check on your bank.
How much did he remit?
You should remit on the first of the month.

subscribe: in this sense, agree to take a share in financing a business operation

Was your bank required to subscribe to any stock?
I haven't decided whether to subscribe.
We'll subscribe the same amount they do.

transit: in this sense, having to do with the collection of checks drawn on other banks

The transit department will send it to the Federal Reserve Bank.
They want to study transit procedures.
Who's in charge of your transit department now?

treasury: any place where valuable things, especially money, are kept; the funds belonging to an organization

They're fiscal agents of the United States Treasury.
How much money is in the treasury?
He says the treasury is getting pretty low.

United States Treasury (Department): the agency which controls the currency and public funds of the United States

They're fiscal agents of the United States Treasury.
Where is the United States Treasury located?
Federal taxes are paid into the United States Treasury.

C. Check-Up

Fill in the blanks with the proper terms from the list.

discount rate	industrial bank
face value	rediscounted
transit	refinancing
fiscal	subscribed
mutual savings bank	United States Treasury

1. When we became a member of the Federal Reserve System, we agreed to take a share in financing the System. We ______ to some stock.
2. The Federal Reserve Banks perform a lot of services for us as representatives of the agency that controls the currency and public funds of the United States. This agency is called the ______.
3. Anything having to do with public funds is a ______ matter.
4. These banks assist us in other ways. If our cash reserve becomes low, they'll accept from us any notes that can be sold at a price less than their value at maturity. They'll accept any notes that can be ______.
5. They help in the issuing of new bonds to replace ones that have matured. They help in ______ bonds that have reached maturity.
6. Many of our dealings with the Federal Reserve Banks concern the clearing of checks. Checks flowing through the System are cleared at the value written on the face of the check. They're cleared at ______.
7. The local bank is borrowing money from the Federal Reserve. The interest rate they pay is called the ______.
8. This bank is owned completely by its depositors. It's a ______.
9. This bank makes loans for the purchase or manufacture of industrial products. It is an ______.
10. The ______ department is responsible for the collection of checks drawn on other banks.

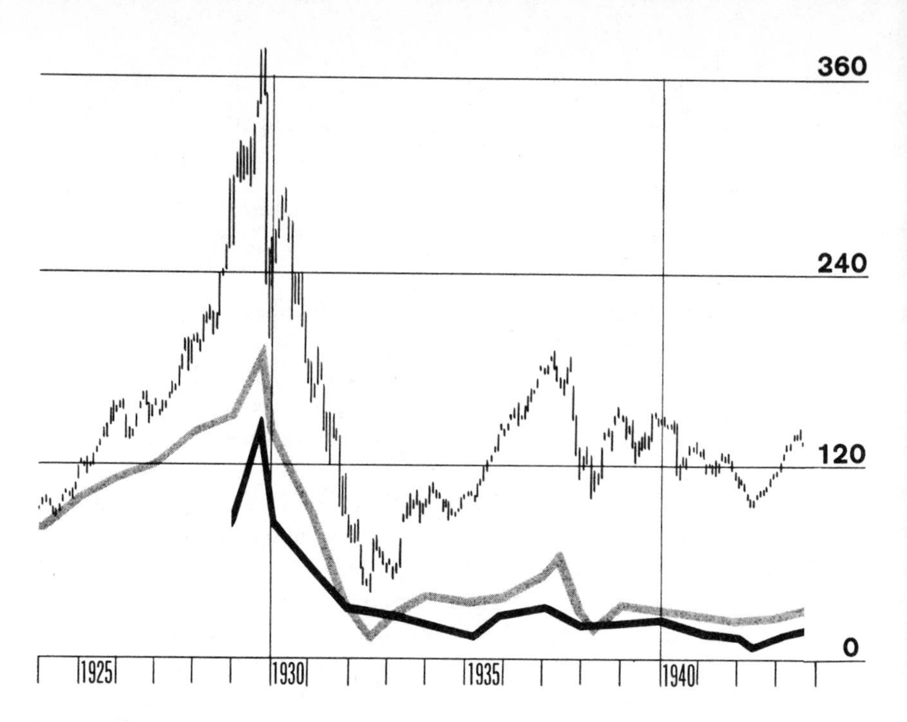

LESSON

13 Government Controls

A. Dialogue

Customer: Why does there have to be so much governmental control of banking?

Banker: Well, of course, the major reason cited for all of these controls is to protect the depositor. By limiting excessive risk taking on the part of banks, for instance, they reduce the chance that the banks will fail and be unable to meet their obligations to their depositors.

Customer: How is the borrower protected by regulation?

Banker: To the extent that regulation prevents monopoly, it reduces the amount a bank may charge on loans.

Customer: This is a protection against usury.

Banker: In an indirect way, yes. Then there are more direct controls that protect both the bank and the customer from loss by embezzlement.

Customer: By an audit of the books?

Banker: Partly. But also by requiring that each employee be bonded.

Customer: Don't these controls have something to do with financial conditions?

Banker: Some of them. As a matter of fact, a large part of existing regulatory controls grew out of the disaster of the Great Depression of the 1930's. After a history of repeated panic that culminated in the Great Depression, it was easy to provide a rationale for regulations and controls. These regulatory measures were designed to build up people's confidence in the economy.

Customer: That was about the time gold was taken out of circulation, wasn't it?

Banker: Yes. We went off the gold standard in 1933.

Customer: Wasn't the Great Depression caused by the crash in 1929?

Banker: Well, it contributed to it. We'd gone through a stock market boom and a period of prosperity, and the people weren't prepared for the shock to the nation's economy.

Customer: There was a panic.

Banker: Yes, a very serious one. There were dangerous runs on banks, and banks had to foreclose on many mortgages.

Customer: It must have been a pretty bad time.

Banker: It was. The FDIC contributed greatly to the remedy of this situation. In fact, many economists now argue that this protection is sufficient.

Customer: There seems to be a trend toward phasing out regulation of the banking system.

Banker: It looks that way. Congressional passage of the Depository Institutions Deregulation and Monetary Control Act of 1980 marks the most important banking legislation since the 1930's.

B. Terminology Practice

bond: in this sense, take out insurance against financial loss caused by the person so insured

There's a requirement that each employee be bonded.
How much is a teller bonded for?
If he gets the job, he'll have to be bonded.

boom: in this sense, a period or condition of very successful business activity

We'd gone through a stock market boom.
We thought we were sitting pretty during the boom.
Some people feel that a crash always follows a boom.

ceiling: in this sense, an upper limit

There are legal ceilings on interest rates.
I expect the ceilings to be lowered.
Is there a ceiling on the interest paid on savings accounts?

circulation: in this sense, the passing (of money) from person to person

Gold was taken out of circulation, wasn't it?
There aren't many of these coins in circulation any more.
When will the new bills be put into circulation?

crash: in this sense, a sudden fall in the market, causing financial ruin to many people

Wasn't the Great Depression caused by the crash in 1929?
They were very nearly wiped out in the crash.
We've been much more careful of our investments since the crash.

deflation: in this sense, a fall in market prices and an increase in the buying power of money

Doesn't the government try to protect the country against deflation?
Deflation is really something that begins in people's minds.
He'd be in bad shape if deflation set in.

depositor: a party who makes deposits

The main objective is to protect the depositor.
The number of our depositors is growing every day.
The FDIC insures depositors against loss.

depression: in this sense, a period or condition of lessening business activity, with falling prices and wages

Didn't the government step in during the Great Depression?
The depression lasted for several years.
He lost all his property during the Great Depression.

economy: in this sense, the financial structure and operations of a country in relation to its wealth and resources

The people weren't prepared for the shock to the nation's economy.
The economy is in very healthy condition.
Investment bankers must keep a sharp eye on the economy.

embezzlement: the theft of money which has been placed in one's care

There are controls that protect the bank from loss by embezzlement.

Aren't the employees bonded to protect the bank against embezzlement?

The examiners discovered a case of embezzlement.

foreclose: take possession of property given as security for a loan because the loan has not been paid as agreed

They had to foreclose on many mortgages they held.

The bank always hesitates to foreclose on a mortgage.

The bank has told him that they'll have to foreclose.

hoarding: in this sense, keeping money in one's own possession and out of circulation

It was necessary to discourage hoarding.

There was a lot of hoarding during the panic.

It's hard to tell how much hoarding is going on.

inefficient: not producing the desired effect with a minimum use of energy

The firm is inefficient.

The worker's inefficiency reduced output.

Inefficiency reduces growth.

inflation: in this sense, a rise in market prices and a decrease in the buying power of money

Doesn't the government try to protect the country against inflation?

The economy is suffering from inflation.

He expects the inflation to level off soon.

monetary: having to do with money

That gets pretty involved in monetary theory.

They're making a study of the monetary situation.

The government's monetary policy has had good results.

monopoly: exclusive control of commodity or service in a given market

Some monopolies are efficient because they're natural monopolies.

Monopolies generally result in a welfare loss.

There are very few real monopolies.

panic: in this sense, a sudden fear among the people of a collapse of the financial system, causing hoarding and a rush to turn property into cash

There was a panic.

During a panic there are always runs on the banks.

The government tried to control the panic.

prosperity: a period or condition of general financial success

We'd gone through a period of prosperity.

The people began to believe that prosperity was coming.

What can be done to bring about prosperity?

run: in this sense, a rush by depositors to remove their funds from a bank

There were dangerous runs on banks.

The bank expected a run and had plenty of cash on hand.

The news caused a run on the bank.

standard: in this sense, a basis for the value of currency

We went off the gold standard in 1933.

What is the monetary standard of that country?

Silver has sometimes been used as a monetary standard.

usury: in this sense, the practice of charging rates of interest that are higher than the fair or legal limits

This is a protection against what they call usury.

The laws against usury are very strict.

He has been accused of usury.

C. Check-Up

Fill in the blanks with the proper terms from the list.

boom	hoarding
crash	panic
depression	prosperity
economy	runs
foreclose	standard

1. Before 1929 there was a period of very successful business activity in the United States. There was a ______.
2. Then, in that year, came a sudden fall in the market, and many people were ruined financially. There was a ______.
3. The people were thrown into a sudden fear that the financial system would collapse. There was a ______.
4. The people began keeping their money in their own possession and out of circulation. They started ______.
5. The depositors rushed to remove their funds from the banks. There were ______ on the banks.
6. The banks had to take possession of property given as security for loans when these loans could not be paid as agreed. They had to ______ on mortgages.
7. At about that time, also, the government declared that gold was no longer the basis for the value of our currency. We went off the gold ______.
8. All this was a great shock to the financial structure and operations of the country. It was a shock to the ______.
9. For several years afterward, there was a period of lessening business activity, with falling prices and wages. There was a ______.
10. At the present time the country is enjoying a period of general financial success. This is a time of ______.

The Eurodollar Market

A. Dialogue

Student: There has been a lot of talk about the rapid growth of the Eurodollar market. What exactly is a Eurodollar?

Banker: A Eurodollar is a dollar deposit outside of the United States. The bank at which it is deposited is called a Eurobank. A Eurobank always deals in currencies other than the legal currency of the country in which it exists. The major distinction between a U.S. dollar deposit and a Eurodollar deposit is that the latter is under little or no regulation by a government's monetary authority. A major impetus to the growth of the Eurodollar market was the 1965 Voluntary Credit Restraint Program (VCRP), which attempted to curtail credits that U.S. banks could extend abroad.

Student: Is it fair to say that Eurobanks have made it more difficult for the Federal Reserve to conduct monetary policy?

Banker: Yes, although people still debate the degree to which this is so. The Eurodollar market often acts as a buffer for counteracting the effects of domestic monetary policy. For example, while the Federal Reserve might be able to reduce the quantity of domestic deposits, the total quantity of dollar deposits might remain unchanged if Eurodollar deposits increased. In order to equalize the Eurodollar market, Regulation M has been enacted.

Student: What are the major Eurocurrencies?

Banker: The dollar, the pound sterling, the deutsche mark, and the Swiss franc. They all share the characteristic of being relatively freely convertible into other currencies.

B. Terminology Practice

convertible: freely exchanged for another currency

The U.S. dollar is probably the most convertible of all currencies.

During the Second World War sterling was inconvertible.

The ruble is not convertible into western currencies.

counteract: to oppose the effects of an action by a contrary action

In an effort to counteract the expansion of the Eurodollar, regulations were imposed.

The Voluntary Credit Restraint Program was initiated to counteract the deterioration of the U.S. balance of payment.

The Fed is attempting to counteract inflation by reducing the rate of growth of the money supply.

Eurocurrencies: currencies held by individuals and institutions outside the country of their origin

The Eurocurrency market often circumvents domestic monetary policy.

The major Eurocurrencies are the U.S. dollar, the pound sterling, the deutsche mark, and the Swiss franc.

The market for Eurocurrencies is not confined to Europe.

monetary authority: that institution responsible for the execution of monetary policy

The Federal Reserve Board is the monetary authority in the U.S.

The monetary authority in the U.S. is constitutionally independent from the executive branch of government.

The monetary authority influences the quantity of money in an economy.

monetary policy: the division of economic policy which regulates the quantity of money in the economy in order to achieve growth, price level stability, and full employment

U.S. monetary policy took a decisively different course in October 1979.

The Federal Reserve conducts U.S. monetary policy.

Some countries have very expansionary monetary policies.

Regulation M: a regulation instituted by the Federal Reserve in 1969 which established reserve requirements on deposits of Eurobank branches at the home office

Regulation M initially set a reserve requirement of ten percent on deposits.

Regulation M probably did retard the Euromarket activity of U.S. banks.

Regulation M made U.S. banks less competitive in Euromarket activity.

Voluntary Credit Restraint Program (VCRP): a program instituted by President Johnson to reduce the outflow of U.S. capital

The VCRP attempted to improve the U.S. balance of payments.

The VCRP escalated the expansion of the Eurodollar market.

Was the VCRP suspended at the end of 1973?

C. Check-Up

Fill in the blanks with the proper terms from the list.

convertible
counteracts
Eurocurrencies
monetary authority
monetary policy
Regulation M
Voluntary Credit Restraint Program

1. The ______ is the executor of monetary policy.
2. ______ was imposed to slow the growth of the Eurodollar market.

3. They ______ attempted to improve the U.S. balance of payments position.
4. The goal of ______ is growth, price level stability, and full employment.
5. Swiss francs can be freely exchanged for U.S. dollars. They are ______ into dollars.
6. Swiss francs, U.S. dollars, deutsche marks, and pound sterling are the major ______.
7. Eurodollar activity often ______ Federal Reserve policy.

Key to Exercises

Lesson 1

1. board of directors
2. stockholders
3. vice-president
4. statement
5. reserves
6. capital
7. dividends
8. profits
9. loan
10. investments

Lesson 2

1. currency
2. cash
3. negotiable
4. denominations
5. check
6. identification
7. in lieu of
8. issued
9. bank draft
10. sight draft

Lesson 3

1. joint account
2. deposits
3. withdrawals
4. balance
5. overdraft
6. statement
7. canceled
8. outstanding
9. service charge
10. reconciled

Lesson 4

1. principal
2. NOW
3. compounded
4. credited
5. FDIC
6. term
7. time deposit
8. maturity
9. rate of interest
10. liquid

Lesson 5

1. credit
2. balance sheet
3. open note
4. current assets
5. collateral
6. pledge
7. fixed assets
8. mortgage
9. amortized
10. liquidate

Lesson 6

1. holdings
2. clear
3. encumbrance
4. real estate
5. net worth
6. secure
7. chattel mortgage
8. trust deed
9. co-signer
10. appraised

Lesson 7

1. stocks
2. fluctuation
3. speculative
4. bonds
5. portfolio
6. diversified
7. issue
8. revenue bonds
9. tax-exempt
10. yield

Lesson 8

1. lending
2. commercial banks
3. national bank
4. Federal Land Bank
5. savings and loan association
6. credit union
7. trust company
8. fiduciary
9. brokerage house
10. securities

Lesson 9

1. will
2. executor
3. safe-deposit box
4. inventory
5. creditors
6. demands
7. beneficiary
8. inheritance
9. probated
10. allowance

Lesson 10

1. shares
2. bid
3. commission
4. market
5. growth
6. flier
7. preferred stocks
8. common stocks
9. redemption
10. proceeds

Lesson 11

1. correspondent banks
2. clearinghouses
3. central banks
4. letters
5. collection
6. commercial paper
7. endorse
8. foreign exchange
9. quotations
10. listed

Lesson 12

1. subscribed
2. United States Treasury
3. fiscal
4. rediscounted
5. refinancing
6. face value
7. discount rate
8. mutual savings bank
9. industrial bank
10. transit

Lesson 13

1. boom
2. crash
3. panic
4. hoarding
5. runs
6. foreclose
7. standard
8. economy
9. depression
10. prosperity

Lesson 14

1. monetary authority
2. Regulation M
3. VRCP
4. monetary policy
5. convertible
6. Eurocurrencies
7. counteracts

Appendix

Although there are many internationally used banking procedures, banking systems differ in some ways from country to country. Even amongst the English-speaking countries there are different ways of referring to the same thing, as well as different means of providing services that are essentially similar. The banking systems, and terminology, in most of the English speaking countries resemble British practice.

Some differences of structure between the U.S. and British banking systems, from examples in this book, are: the Bank of England has the functions of the Federal Reserve System and the National Banks, and is the only "central" bank (although the leading British commercial banks have organized a central clearing-house and made local arrangements to clear checks collected on behalf of one another). There is no equivalent of the F.D.I.C., British banks making their own insurance arrangements; there is no equivalent of the Federal Land Bank, and, of course, no State Banks. In Britain, only the Bank of England has a government charter; other banks are limited companies or partnerships. The larger British commercial banks (generally, limited companies) deal with tax, trust, succession and investment matters as well as with receipts and payments (e.g. Midland Bank Executor and Trustee Co., Ltd., Barclays Bank Ltd., Trustee Department) etc.; there are no separate Trust Companies.

Other differences, of word or method, are noted in the list below. This gives first, in alphabetical order, the term used in this book and then notes the equivalent British words or practice.

AA rating—A1, first-class

amortized—repaid by annual installments

bill—note

brokerage house—firm of (stock) brokers

cashier—accountant; chief clerk

cashier's check—*no equivalent*

chattel mortgage—charge on goods or effects

checking account—current account

commercial paper—money at short notice (e.g., investment in Treasury bills)

corporate bond—corporation, or local government, stock

coupon type—bearer (unregistered)

bonding employees—*this practice seems to be dying out in British banks*

correspondent bank—*usually foreign banks acting on behalf of the home bank; not in general use among British banks*

discount committee—*no equivalent: Small loans or overdrafts are at the discretion of the branch manager; for larger ones, permission from Head Office (Loans and Overdrafts Department) is necessary*

examiners—inspectors *(employed by the bank, not the government)*

installment loan—*no equivalent*

Municipal Bond Offering—Local Government Loan Issue

mutual savings bank—*no direct equivalent: Nearest is Building Society (see Savings and Loan Association)*

note—loan (due for repayment)

open note—unsecured loan, contract or agreement

President (*of bank*)—*usually*, Chairman

Vice-President *(of bank)*—Vice-Chairman or Managing Director

real estate (ie. freehold or leasehold)—freehold property

rediscount—discount

savings account—deposit account

Savings and Loan Association—Building Society

service charge—commission (or charge)

silver certificate—silver, cupro-nickel and copper coins

statement (*of bank's financial condition*)—balance sheet (or statement)

stockholder—shareholder

surplus—*no equivalent: "Reserves" cover all proprietors' capital except nominal share capital issued*

time deposit—*no direct equivalent: Withdrawals from deposit accounts are all technically subject to notice*

teller—cashier

teller's cage—cashier's till

trust deed—legal charge

vault—vault, strongroom

Glossary

Key to references: (2) = lesson 2

AA rating (7) a high estimate of the value of a bond or stock; the ratings are made impartially by a company whose speciality is evaluation of investments

account (1) in this sense, a record of financial transactions; money on deposit in a bank

active (3) in this sense, frequently used

allowance (9) in this sense, an amount of money regularly given to a person for current expenses

amortize (5) make regular payments on the principal as well as the interest

appraise (6) judge the value of

asset (5) anything owned that has financial value

assign (10) in this sense, transfer ownership

balance (3) in this sense, the amount remaining in an account

balance sheet (5) a brief statement of a party's financial condition

bank draft (2) a type of exchange; a document whereby a bank requests another bank to accept liability for making payment

bank money order (2) a type of exchange; a bank's unqualified promise to pay a specified sum to a specific individual or corporation, sold by the bank against payment of cash

bank note (2) currency issued to a bank by the Federal Reserve Banks

bearer (2) the person who is named as payee in a piece of exchange, or who presents it for payment

beneficiary (9) the party to whom property or a sum of money is given under the terms of a will or trust

benefits (9) in this sense, payments

bid (10) in this sense, make an offer to buy at a certain price

bill (2) in this sense, a piece of paper currency

blue chip (7) a stock thought to be of highest quality

board of directors (1) a group of people who control the activities of a bank or company

bond (7) in this sense, a unit of fixed obligation of a company or government for a fixed term

(13) in this sense, take out insurance against financial loss caused by the person so insured

boom (13) in this sense, a period or condition of very successful business activity

broker (8) a person who sells or buys stocks and bonds for others

brokerage (8) the buying and selling of stock and bonds for other persons

brokerage house (8) an institution which handles brokerage

canceled (3) in this sense, stamped to indicate that payment has been made

capital (1) in this sense, the money used to start a bank or company

cash (2) change into currency
(7) coins and bills

cashier (1) an officer of a bank in charge of the money which goes in and out of a bank or company

cashier's check (2) a negotiable form of exchange issued by a bank to a specific order and endorsed by an officer of the bank

cash-in-banks (7) cash kept in other banks as a reserve

ceiling (13) in this sense, an upper limit

central bank (11) a bank which regulates the supply of currency within an area, also serving as a clearinghouse

certificate (2) a written statement given or held as proof of something

certified check (2) a type of exchange; a check drawn by an account holder and certified by the bank that funds are available

certify (2) guarantee the truth or worth of something

charter (1) in this sense, permission granted by the government to do business

chattel (6) any personal or movable possession, such as furniture or equipment

chattel mortgage (6) a mortgage on chattels

check (2) in this sense, a written order to a bank to pay the stated amount of money

checking account (1) an account in a bank from which money can be drawn by check

circulation (13) in this sense, the passing (of money) from person to person

clear (6) in this sense, without encumbrance
(11) in this sense, pass through a clearinghouse

clearinghouse (11) an office where banks exchange checks drawn on one another

clerical (1) having to do with the keeping of records and with correspondence

coin (2) a piece of currency made of metal

collateral (5) anything pledged as security for a loan

collection (11) in this sense, the process of obtaining payment of an item of exchange

commercial bank (8) a bank whose major services are accepting and protecting money for depositors and paying checks issued by the depositors; laws permit it to invest for profit a portion of this money

commercial paper (11) short-term obligations of industrial companies

commission (10) in this sense, a charge for services in a sale, based on the amount of the transaction

common stock (10) ordinary stock, with no fixed dividend rate

compound (4) in this sense, figure interest on the principal plus any accrued interest

convertible (14) freely exchanged for another currency

corporate bond (10) a bond issued by a corporation, or group of people who have a charter to act as an individual

correspondent bank (11) a bank with which another bank has regular dealings

co-signer (6) a person who signs a document with another person and shares the obligation

counseling (9) having to do with giving advice

counteract (14) to oppose the effects of an action by a contrary action

coupon (10) in this sense, removable printed statement on a bond of the interest due at a particular time—it must be presented for collection

crash (13) in this sense, a sudden fall in the market, causing financial ruin to many people

credit (4) in this sense, add to an account; enter in a ledger so that the balance is increased

credit (5) in this sense, permission to borrow money as the need arises

creditor (9) a party to whom a debt is owed

credit union (8) an institution formed by a group of persons who combine their savings in order to make loans to members at a low rate of interest

currency (2) in this sense, money issued by the government for general use

current assets (5) assets other than real estate which can be readily changed into money

debenture (11) an obligation issued by a corporation which pays interest but is often unsecured

debit (3) *n.*, a figure in a ledger indicating a withdrawal or a charge; *v.*, to deduct from an account

debt (5) anything owed

deed (6) in this sense, a document which proves a change of ownership of real estate

deflation (13) in this sense, a fall in market prices and an increase in the buying power of money

demand (9) in this sense, a request for payment

denomination (2) in this sense, unit of value

deposit (3) money put into an account

depositor (13) a party who makes deposits

depression (13) in this sense, a period or condition of lessening business activity, with falling prices and wages

discount (5) in this sense, having to do with making loans and purchasing investments at a price below their maturity value so that a profit can be made

discount rate (12) the interest rate that the Federal Reserve charges when it lends to member banks

diversified (7) in this sense, made up of a variety of stocks and bonds

dividend (1) a sum of money paid to a stockholder or shares of stock issued to him out of profits in relation to his investment

drawee (12) the bank on whom an item of exchange is drawn

economy (13) in this sense, the financial structure and operations of a country in relation to its wealth and resources

embezzlement (13) the theft of money which has been placed in one's care

empower (9) give power to

encumbrance (6) in this sense, an indebtedness, such as a mortgage

endorse (11) in this sense, place one's signature on the back of a document in order to transfer ownership

endorse with recourse (12) endorse with the understanding that one is liable for payment if other parties to the transaction refuse payment

equity (6) in this sense, the value of a piece of property beyond any indebtedness held against it

equity/deposit ratio (7) total assets minus total liabilities divided by deposits

estate (6) in this sense, the holdings and obligations left by a dead person

estimate (6) judge the value of

Eurocurrencies (14) currencies held by individuals and institutions outside the country of their origin

excess reserves (7) reserves in excess of the legal requirement against bank liabilities

exchange (2) in this sense, a means of transferring money; anything with money value used in such an action

(8) in this sense, a place where business transactions are made

executor (9) a party appointed to carry out the requests in a will

face value (12) the value printed on the bill or other instrument

Federal Deposit Insurance Corporation (FDIC) (4) an agency of the government of the United States that insures up to $40,000 of the account of each depositor in state and national banks

federal land bank (8) a bank established by the government of the United States to make loans for the purchase of land

Federal Reserve System (2) a banking system set up by the government of the United States to regulate currency and banking policies

fiduciary (8) having to do with a trust

financial intermediary (8) a financial institution that acts as a middleman, transferring funds from ultimate lenders to ultimate borrowers

fiscal (12) in this sense, having to do with public funds

fixed asset (5) an asset, such as real estate which cannot be readily changed into money

flier (10) in this sense, a speculative transaction

fluctuation (7) a changing back and forth

foreclose (13) take possession of property given as security for a loan because the loan has not been paid as agreed

foreign exchange (11) any item of exchange from another nation

funds (4) money

general obligation bond (7) a bond secured by all the property of a city or other unit of government

genuine (3) true, actually being what it appears to be

growth (10) in this sense, giving promise of development, so that the value of an investment will increase

hoarding (13) in this sense, keeping money in one's own possession and out of circulation

holding (6) something owned, such as property or securities

identification (2) proof that a person is who he or she claims to be

income (9) earnings

incorporated (12) having a charter to act as an individual

indebtedness (5) debt

industrial bank (12) a bank which makes loans for the purchase or manufacture of industrial products, using a repayment plan of certificate purchases by installment which permits higher legal rates of interest than on other loans

inefficient (13) not producing the desired effect with the minimum use of energy

inflation (13) in this sense, a rise in market prices and a decrease in the buying power of money

inheritance (9) money or property received from an estate

in lieu of (2) instead of

installment (11) in this sense, one of several payments on an obligation

insurance (4) protection against loss

inventory (9) a list of items of property

invest (1) put money into a business in order to make profit

investment (1) money put into a business in order to make profit; the act of doing this

issue (2) in this sense, prepare and give out
(7) in this sense, all the stock or bonds offered for sale at one time by a particular company or government

joint account (3) an account held in the names of two or more persons

ledger (3) a book in which records of accounts are kept

legal tender (2) money guaranteed by a government

lending (8) in this sense, empowered to make loans

letter (11) in this sense, the items of exchange presented by or to a correspondent bank for collection on a particular day

liability (5) in this sense, any financial obligation

liable (12) in this sense, required to make payment

life insurance (9) a sum of money payable in case of loss of life

liquid (4) in this sense, readily changeable into money

liquidate (5) in this sense, pay off

listed (11) in this sense, accepted for sale on a stock exchange

loan (1) in this sense, money which one person allows another to use for a specified time and which will be returned with an additional payment for its use; the act of giving out such money

market (10) in this sense, the buying and selling which is taking place at any one time

mature (10) in this sense, become due for payment

maturity (4) in this sense, the point at which a loan or investment is due

monetary (13) having to do with money

monetary authority (14) that institution responsible for the execution of monetary policy which regulates the quantity of money in the economy in order to achieve growth, price level stability, and full employment

monopoly (13) exclusive control of commodity or service in a given market

mortgage (5) an agreement to give up the collateral which has been pledged if a debt is not paid

municipal bond (7) a bond offered for sale by a city or other unit of government

mutual (12) in this sense, having a structure of shared ownership by those who make use of the institution

mutual savings bank (12) a savings bank which is owned by the depositors

national bank (8) a bank which has a charter from the federal government

negotiable (2) able to be given over to another party

Negotiable Order of Withdrawal (NOW) account (4) interest bearing-checking account

net (6) in this sense, the amount remaining after all expenses or obligations have been subtracted

net worth (6) the value of one's holdings after all obligations have been subtracted

note (5) in this sense, an agreement between a borrower and a lender; the written promise to repay a loan

notice (4) in this sense, an announcement

obligation (5) in this sense, an indebtedness one must repay

offering (7) in this sense, a quantity of stocks or bonds offered for sale at one time

open note (5) a note, the payment of which is not guaranteed by collateral security

outstanding (3) in this sense, written but not yet presented for payment by the bank

overdraft (3) an amount by which withdrawals are greater than the balance in an account

panic (13) in this sense, a sudden fear among the people of a collapse of the financial system, causing hoarding and a rush to turn property into cash

paper (11) in this sense, any written promise to pay

par (1) in this sense, the value printed on the face of a certificate of obligation

party (1) in this sense, a person or association that enters into an agreement with another

passbook (4) a small book held by a savings account customer in which each deposit and withdrawal is entered

pledge (5) in this sense, promise as security

policy (9) in this sense, an insurance contract; a certificate of such a contract

portfolio (7) in this sense, a list of stocks and bonds belonging to one holder

posting (3) in this sense, recording figures in a ledger

preferred stock (10) stock on which dividends are paid before those on common stock and which gives the holder some rights to any assets that are distributed

president (1) the officer who has the major responsibility for the management of a business

principal (4) in this sense, the unpaid balance or portion of a loan or investment, on which the interest is figured

probate (9) prove (a will) genuine and place on the records of the proper court

proceeds (10) the money received from some transaction

profit (1) earnings remaining after all the expenses of a business activity have been paid

property (6) in this sense, anything owned, especially real estate or land

prosperity (13) a period or condition of general financial success

quarterly (4) four times a year

quotation (11) in this sense, a statement of the current price

rate of interest (4) the percentage paid for the use of money

real estate (6) land, including anything constructed on it

reconcile (3) in this sense, compare and make to agree

recourse (12) *see: endorse with recourse*

redemption (10) in this sense, the collection at maturity of money invested in a bond

red tape (12) the use of official forms and procedures that impede efficiency

refinancing (12) issuing a new obligation to replace an older one

registered (10) in this sense, having the owner's name placed on a record and on the certificate

Regulation M (14) a regulation instituted by the Federal Reserve in 1969 which established reserve requirements on deposits of Eurobank branches at the home office

remit (12) send or pay (money)

reserves (1) in this sense, earnings kept back for later use

retire (5) in this sense, pay off

revenue (7) in this sense, money earned by a government especially for performance of a public service

revenue bond (7) a bond which is repaid out of revenues

run (13) in this sense, a rush by depositors to remove their funds from a bank

safe-deposit box (9) a locked box for important papers, usually kept in a bank

savings account (1) an account in a bank on which the depositor receives interest

savings and loan association (8) an institution which accepts savings deposits and makes loans mainly for the purchase and repair of homes

seat (10) in this sense, the right to take part as a member

secure (6) *v.*, in this sense, to guarantee payment of

security (5) in this sense, a guarantee of payment
(8) in this sense, a stock or bond

service charge (3) in this sense, a fee collected by a bank for its checking account services

sight draft (2) a form of request for payment through a bank

signature (3) a person's name as he or she writes it

silver certificate (2) a type of paper currency

share (10) in this sense, a unit of ownership in a company

speculative (7) in this sense, bought and sold in an attempt to make profits from price fluctuations

standard (13) in this sense, a basis for the value of currency

state bank (8) a bank which has a charter from a state agency

statement (1) in this sense, an announcement of a bank's financial condition

(3) in this sense, a record of a customer's deposits and withdrawals

stock (7) in this sense, a unit of ownership in a company

stock exchange (8) a place where stocks are bought and sold

stockholder (1) a party who holds part ownership in a company

subscribe (12) in this sense, agree to take a share in financing a business operation

surplus (1) money owned by a company in addition to its capital

tax (7) money collected by a government for its support

tax-exempt (7) free from tax obligation

teller (1) an employee in a bank who pays out and receives money

term (4) in this sense, a period of time

terms (9) in this sense, stated conditions, as in a will or contract

time certificate (4) a certificate given to one who makes a time deposit

time deposit (4) a savings deposit made for a specified term

title (6) in this sense, the record or proof of ownership of property

transaction (8) a business action

transferable (4) able to be signed over to another person

transit (12) in this sense, having to do with the collection of checks drawn on other banks

traveler's check (2) a check issued by a bank or other qualified corporation in a fixed denomination and becoming negotiable upon endorsement by the purchaser

treasury (12) any place where valuable things, especially money, are kept; the funds belonging to an organization

trust (6) in this sense, the legal responsibility given to one party to act for another in financial matters

trust company (8) an institution which manages trusts and estates

trust deed (6) a deed to real estate held as security for a loan—in effect, a mortgage

trustee (9) a party to whom a trust is given

undivided profits (1) profits not yet paid out as dividends or added to the surplus

United States Treasury (Department) (12) the agency which controls the currency and public funds of the United States

usury (13) in this sense, the practice of charging rates of interest that are higher than the fair or legal limits

variance of demand deposits (7) the degree of fluctuation in the inflows and outflows of demand deposits (checking accounts)

vice-president (1) an officer in a company who assists the president

Voluntary Credit Restraint Program (VCRP) (14) a program instituted by President Johnson whose central focus was measured to reduce the outflow of U.S. capital

will (9) a document which states how a person wishes his estate to be divided, made public only after his death

withdrawal (3) money removed from an account; the act of removing it

yield (7) in this sense, earn

NOTES